SECOND EDITION

TOP NOTCH

English for Today's World

FUNDAMENTALS

Joan Saslow • Allen Ascher

With *Top Notch Pop Songs and Karaoke*
by Rob Morsberger

Top Notch: English for Today's World Fundamentals, Second Edition

Pearson Education, 10 Bank Street, White Plains, NY 10606

Staff credits: The people who made up the *Top Notch Fundamentals* team—representing editorial, design, production, and manufacturing—are Rhea Banker, Elizabeth Carlson, Aerin Csigay, Mindy DePalma, Dave Dickey, Warren Fischbach, Aliza Greenblatt, Ray Keating, Mike Kemper, Maria Pia Marrella, Jessica Miller-Smith, Barbara Sabella, Martin Yu, and Wendy Wolf.

Cover design: Rhea Banker
Cover photo: Sprint/Corbis
Text design: Elizabeth Carlson
Text composition: Quarasan!

Library of Congress Cataloging-in-Publication Data

Saslow, Joan M.

  Top notch : English for today's world / Joan Saslow, Allen Ascher ; with Top Notch pop songs and Karaoke by
  Rob Morsberger. — 2nd ed.
    p. cm.
  ISBN 0-13-246988-X (set) — ISBN 0-13-247038-1 (v. 1) — ISBN 0-13-247048-9 (v. 2) — ISBN 0-13-247027-6
  (v. 3) 1. English language — Textbooks for foreign speakers. 2. English language — Problems, exercises, etc.
  I. Ascher, Allen. II. Title.
  PE1128.S2757 2011
  428.2′4 — dc22

                    2010019162

Photo credits: All original photography by Sharon Hoogstraten and David Mager. Page 4 (1) nikkytok/Shutterstock, (2) Dex Images/Corbis, (3) Royalty-Free/Corbis, (4) Mark Richards/PhotoEdit, Inc., (5) Jim Arbogast/Getty Images, (6) Getty Images, (7) James P. Blair/Corbis, (8) Spencer Grant/PhotoEdit, Inc., (9) Kevin Winter/Getty Images, (10) Reuters NewMedia Inc./Corbis; p. 5 (left) AP Images/Chris Polk, (middle left) Alexander Tamargo/Getty Images, (middle right) Courtesy of Korean Concert Society, (right) AP Images/Petr David Josek; p. 6 (1) Alan Bolesta/Index Stock Imagery, (2) Kim Steele/Getty Images, (3) Tom McCarthy/PhotoEdit, Inc., (4) Thinkstock, (5) JPC-PROD/Fotolia, (6) Getty Images, (7) Getty Images, (8) Getty Images, p. 8 (top) Shutterstock.com; p. 10 (left) Robert Mora/Getty Images, (middle left) Kabik/Retna Ltd./Corbis, (middle right) Reuters NewMedia Inc./Corbis, (right) Piero Pomponi/Liaison/Getty Images; p. 13 (top) Shutterstock.com; (1) Shutterstock.com, (2) Shutterstock.com, (3) Shutterstock.com, p. 16 (left) Shutterstock.com; p. 18 (Gehry) Thierry Prat/Sygma/Corbis, (de Lucia) Alonso Gonzales/Reuters/Corbis, (Sharapova) Reuters/Corbis, (Travolta) AP Images/Rob Griffith, (Kidjo) Michael Latz AFP/Getty Images, (Yoshimoto) Tiziana Fabi/AFP/Getty Images; p. 19 (background) iStockphoto.com; p. 20 (1) Bill Aron/PhotoEdit, Inc., (2) Getty Images, (3) Steven Dunwell/Getty Images, (4) Shutterstock.com, (5) Jeff Greenberg/PhotoEdit, Inc., (6) Dave Bartruff/Corbis; p. 22 (1) Shutterstock.com, (2) Shutterstock.com, (3) NRT-Travel/Alamy, (4) Shutterstock.com, (5) Shutterstock.com; p. 24 (1) Shutterstock.com, (2) Shutterstock.com, (3) Shutterstock.com, (4) Shutterstock.com, (5) Shutterstock; p. 26 (Lee) Shutterstock.com, (Beck) Shutterstock.com, (White) Shutterstock.com; p. 28 (background) Shutterstock.com, (1 left) Shutterstock.com, (1 right) Shutterstock.com, (2 left) Shutterstock.com, (2 right) Shutterstock.com, (3 left) Shutterstock.com, (3 right) Shutterstock.com, (4 left) Shutterstock.com, (4 right) Shutterstock.com, (5 left) Shutterstock.com, (5 right) Shutterstock.com, (6 left) Shutterstock.com, (6 right) Shutterstock.com; p. 29 Shutterstock.com; p. 30 (1) Douglas Kirkland/Corbis, (2) Lisa O'Connor/ZUMA/Corbis, (4) Melissa Gunn, (7&8) Shutterstock.com, (bottom 2) Arturo Piñango, (bottom 3) Shutterstock.com; p. 31 (4) Antony Nagelmann/Getty Images; p. 32 (top) Shutterstock.com, (buttons) iStockphoto.com; p. 33 (top) Picture Partners/Alamy; p. 34 (left) Reuters NewMedia Inc./Corbis, (middle) Angela Weiss/Getty Images, (right) Vera Anderson/Getty Images; p. 35 (top) David Lok/SuperStock, (bottom) Darama/Corbis; p. 38 (1) Alamy, (2) Rick Gomez/Corbis, (3) AFP/Corbis, (4) Douglas Kirkland/Corbis, (5 inset) Original Films/The Kobal Collection, (6) Graham French/Masterfile, (6) Stephane Cardinale/People Avenue/Corbis, (pants) Fotolia.com, (dance) Chuck Savage/Corbis, (game) Shutterstock.com, (movie) Fox Searchlight/Photofest, (concert) Shutterstock.com; p. 41 (top) Stephanie Maze/Corbis; p. 42 (1-4) Gilbert Duclos; p. 43 (left) EyeWire Collection/Getty Images, (middle) Shutterstock.com, (right) Solus-Veer/Corbis; p. 44 (1) Shutterstock.com, (2) Dorling Kindersley, (3) iStockphoto.com, (4) Jonathan Kantor/Getty Images, (5) FashionSyndicatePress.com, (6) Shutterstock.com, (7) Ryan McVay/Getty Images, (8 left) (5) FashionSyndicatePress.com, (8 right) Shutterstock.com, (9) Getty Images; p. 46 (left) Getty Images; p. 47 (left background) Shutterstock.com, (right background) Shutterstock.com, (pants) Fotolia.com, (tie) Shutterstock.com, (suit) Dorling Kindersley, (sweater) Shutterstock.com, (two-piece) Dorling Kindersley, (shoes) Michael Newman/PhotoEdit, Inc.; p. 48 (1) Shutterstock.com, (2) Shutterstock.com, (4) iStockphoto.com, (7) Shutterstock.com, (8) Shutterstock.com, (9) Comstock Images/Getty Images, (10) Shutterstock.com; p. 49 Jupiterimages/BananaStock/Alamy; p. 50 (red shoes) Shutterstock.com, (purple shoes) Shutterstock.com, (brown shoes) Shutterstock.com; p. 58 (top) Courtesy iRobot Corporation, (middle) Courtesy iRobot Corporation, (left) Reuters/Toshiyuki Aizawa, (bottom) Zucchetti Centro Sistemi spa, (bottom background) Shutterstock.com; p. 59 (top background) Shutterstock.com, (bottom background) Shutterstock.com; p. 63 (middle) Chuck Savage/Corbis; p. 65 (1) John Elk III, (2) Shutterstock.com, (3) William Taufic/Corbis, (4) Dave G. Houser/Corbis, (5) Shutterstock.com, (6) Mimmo Jodice/Corbis, (7) James Leynse/Corbis, (8) Shutterstock.com; p. 69 (leather chair) LonHarding.com, (seat) Shutterstock.com, (lamp) Shutterstock.com, (rug) Jacqui Hurst/Corbis, (sofa) Christie's Images Inc., (stove) Shutterstock.com; p. 70 (background) Shutterstock.com; p. 75 (top) Shutterstock.com; p. 78 (top) Shutterstock.com; p. 81 (bean salad) Shutterstock.com, (soup) Getty Images, (pancakes) Getty Images, (peppers) Fotolia.com; p. 92 (1) Bill Bachmann/Mira.com, (2) Michael Keller/Corbis, (3) Getty Images, (4) Norbert Schaefer/Corbis, (5) Tim Kiusalaas/Corbis, (6) Alamy; p. 94 (top) Shutterstock.com, (middle) iStockphoto.com, (bottom) iStockphoto.com; p. 96 (3) Getty Images, (5) Getty Images, (6) Getty Images, (bottom left) Shutterstock.com, (bottom right) Shutterstock.com; p. 97 (Sangalo) Simon Frederick/Getty Images, (Boccelli) Mencarini/Grazia Neri/Corbis Sygma, (Depardieu) Eric Fougere/VIP Images/Corbis, (Pei) Owen Franken/Corbis, (Roberts) Andrea Renault/Globe Photos; p. 98 (hand) Shutterstock.com, (foot) iStockphoto.com; p. 100 (1) Shutterstock.com, (2) Jupiterimages/Getty Images, (3) Shutterstock.com, (4 left) Shutterstock.com, (4 right) Shutterstock.com; p. 102 (top left) Christopher Morris/Black Star, (bottom left) Alexander Tamargo/Getty Images, (middle) Frank Trapper/Corbis, (right) AP Images/Jan Bauer; p. 105 (top left) Rose Coen, (top right) Shutterstock.com; p. 107 (middle left) Andersen Ross/Getty Images, (middle right) AFP/Corbis, (bottom left) Bill Bachmann/Mira.com, (bottom middle) Norbert Schaefer/Corbis, (bottom right) Stephanie Maze/Corbis; p. 113 (1) Peter Beck/Corbis, (2) ATC Productions/Corbis, (3) Corbis Flirt/Alamy, (4) Chris Ryan/Alamy, (5) Tom & Dee Ann McCarthy/Corbis, (6) Alexander Raths/Fotolia, (7) Monty Rakusen/Getty Images, (8) Shutterstock.com, (9) Michael Keller/Corbis, (10) Billy E. Barnes/PhotoEdit, Inc.; p. 115 (drive) Alamy, (clean) Shutterstock.com, (fish) Shutterstock.com, (TV) Shutterstock.com, (hammock) Shutterstock.com; p. 116 (1) iStockphoto.com, (2) Jade Lee/Asia Images Group, (3) Michael Newman/PhotoEdit Inc., (4 left) Shutterstock.com, (4 right) Dreamstime.com; p. 118 (left) Corbis, (right) Bettmann/Corbis; p. 119 (top) Ron Chapple/Getty Images, (middle left) Image Source/Corbis; p. 126 (3a) Shutterstock.com, (3b) Shutterstock.com, (4a) Shutterstock.com, (4b) James Leynse/Corbis, (5a) Getty Images, (5b) Mimmo Jodice/Corbis; p. 126 (2) Comstock Images/Thinkstock, (3) Keith Brofsky/Getty Images, (4) Arthur S. Aubry/Getty Images, (5) Royalty-Free/Corbis, (6) Shutterstock, (9) Kwame Kikomo/Superstock, (10) Royalty-Free/Corbis, (12) Jonathan Nouvok/The Image Works, (16) Comstock Images, (17) Getty Images, (18) Royalty-Free/Corbis; p. 127 (top left to right) Corbis, Doug Pensinger/Getty Images, Royalty-Free/Corbis, John Henley/Corbis, iStockphoto.com, (4) Vittoriano Rastelli/Corbis, (5) Corbis, (6) Corbis, (7) Corbis, (8) Tom & Dee Ann McCarthy/Corbis, (9) Tom Wagner/Corbis Saba, (10) Jeff Greenberg/PhotoEdit, Inc., (11) Getty Images, (12) Michael Newman/PhotoEdit, Inc., (13) Bill Bachmann/PhotoEdit, Inc., (14) Tom Carter/PhotoEdit, Inc., (15) Jeff Greenberg/PhotoEdit, Inc., p. 128 (top 1) Dorling Kindersley, (top 2) Duane Rieder, (top 3) Dorling Kindersley, (1) Dorling Kindersley, (2) Corbis, (3) Dorling Kindersley, (4) Kazuhiro Nogi/AFP/Getty Images, (5) Robbie Jack Photography, (6) Getty Images; p. 129 (3) Dorling Kindersley, (4) Comstock, (bottom 1) Robert Brenner/PhotoEdit, Inc.; p. 130 (19) Dorling Kindersley; p. 131 (top 1) A&J Verkaik/Corbis, (top 2) Michael S. Yamashita/Corbis, (top 3) Annie Griffiths Belt/National Geographic Image Collection, (top 4) Frozen Images/The Image Works, (bottom) Dennis MacDonald/PhotoEdit, Inc.; p. 133 (2) Royalty-Free/Corbis, (3) Comstock Images, (4) Jim Cummins/Getty Images, (5) Royalty-Free/Corbis, (7) Royalty-Free/Corbis, (8) Royalty-Free/Corbis, (bottom right) Dorling Kindersley; p. 134 (1-10, 12) Dorling Kindersley, (11) Getty Images; p. 135 (1 top) Douglas Faulkner/Corbis, (2 top) Rich Iwasaki/age fotostock, (3 top) Phil Schermeister/Corbis, (4 top) Francoise DeMulder/Corbis, (5 top) Jennifer W. Lester, (6 top) Andrew Douglas/Masterfile, (1) Royalty-Free/Corbis, (2) Pixtal/SuperStock, (3) Royalty-Free/Corbis, (4) Tony Anderson/Getty Images, (5) Gisela Damm/eStock Photo, (6) ThinkStock/SuperStock; p. 146 Comstock Images/Getty Images; p. 147 (middle) Shutterstock.com.

Illustration credits: Kenneth Batelman: pp. 37 (bottom-center), 48 (top), 61, 64, 65, 66; John Ceballos: pp. 43, 51, 67, 95, 120 (top); Pascal DeJong: pp. 11, 87; Karen Donnelly: p. 111; Bob Doucet: p. 27, 119; Len Ebert: p. 110 (right); Ingo Fast: p. 21 (top); Scott Fray: pp. 53, 68, 80, 83; Brian Hughes: pp. 22, 25 (bottom), 36 (top), 46, 89, 92; Robert Kemp: p. 20; Jim Kopp: p. 24; Adam Larkum: p. 103; Pat Lewis: p. 57 (right); Mona Mark: p. 86; Robert McPhillips: p. 119; Suzanne Morgensen: p. 45 (bottom); Andy Myer: pp. 7, 17; Sandy Nichols: pp. 10, 37 (top), 75; NSV Productions: p. 37 (bottom-left, bottom-right); Dusan Petricic: pp. 44, 45 (top), 60 (bottom), 72, 96, 112; Phil Scheuer: pp. 2, 25 (top), 54, 56, 57, 104 (top-right), 106, 114; Steven Stankiewicz: p. 21 (bottom); Don Stewart: p. 48 (center, bottom); Neil Stewart: p. 36 (center-right); Meryl Treatner: p. 37 (center), 110 (top, left); AnnaVeltfort: pp. 12, 52, 74 (top), 104, 106 (1-3 bottom), 108, 120 (bottom), 122; Patrick Welsh: p. 71; XNR Productions: pp. 36 (bottom), 60 (top).

Text credit: Recipes on page 86: Copyright © 1997 by Rozanne Gold. Reprinted by permission of Paradigm Talent and Literary Agency, on behalf of the Author.

Printed in the United States of America

ISBN-10: 0-13-245557-9
ISBN-13: 978-0-13-245557-2
10—V082—17 16 15 14 13

ISBN-10: 0-13-246988-X (with MyEnglishLab)
ISBN-13: 978-0-13-246988-3 (with MyEnglishLab)
5 6 7 8 9 10—V082—17 16 15 14

About the Authors

Joan Saslow

Joan Saslow has taught in a variety of programs in South America and the United States. She is author of a number of multi-level integrated-skills courses for adults and young adults: *Ready to Go: Language, Lifeskills, and Civics; Workplace Plus: Living and Working in English;* and of *Literacy Plus*. She is also author of *English in Context: Reading Comprehension for Science and Technology*. Ms. Saslow was the series director of *True Colors* and *True Voices*. She participates in the English Language Specialist Program in the U.S. Department of State's Bureau of Educational and Cultural Affairs.

Allen Ascher

Allen Ascher has been a teacher and a teacher trainer in China and the United States and taught in the TESOL Certificate Program at the New School in New York. He was also academic director of the International English Language Institute at Hunter College. Mr. Ascher is author of the "Teaching Speaking" module of *Teacher Development Interactive*, an online multimedia teacher-training program, and of *Think about Editing: A Grammar Editing Guide for ESL*.

Both Ms. Saslow and Mr. Ascher are frequent and popular speakers at professional conferences and international gatherings of FFL and ESL teachers.

Authors' Acknowledgments

The authors are indebted to these reviewers who provided extensive and detailed feedback and suggestions for the second edition of *Top Notch* as well as the hundreds of teachers who participated in surveys and focus groups.

Manuel Aguilar Díaz, El Cultural Trujillo, Peru • **Manal Al Jordi**, Expression Training Company, Kuwait • **José Luis Ames Portocarrero**, El Cultural Arequipa, Peru • **Vanessa de Andrade**, CCBEU Inter Americano, Curitiba, Brazil • **Rossana Aragón Castro**, ICPNA Cusco, Peru • **Jennifer Ballesteros**, Universidad del Valle de México, Campus Tlalpan, Mexico City, Mexico • **Brad Bawtinheimer**, PROULEX, Guadalajara, Mexico • **Carolina Bermeo**, Universidad Central, Bogotá, Colombia • **Zulma Buitrago**, Universidad Pedagógica Nacional, Bogotá, Colombia • **Fabiola R. Cabello**, Idiomas Católica, Lima, Peru • **Emma Campo Collante**, Universidad Central Bogotá, Colombia • **Viviane de Cássia Santos Carlini**, Spectrum Line, Pouso Alegre, Brazil • **Fanny Castelo**, ICPNA Cusco, Peru • **José Luis Castro Moreno**, Universidad de León, Mexico • **Mei Chia-Hong**, Southern Taiwan University (STUT), Taiwan • **Guven Ciftci**, Faith University, Turkey • **Freddy Correa Montenegro**, Centro Colombo Americano, Cali, Colombia • **Alicia Craman de Carmand**, Idiomas Católica, Lima, Peru • **Jesús G. Díaz Osío**, Florida National College, Miami, USA • **Ruth Domínguez**, Universidad Central Bogotá, Colombia • **Roxana Echave**, El Cultural Arequipa, Peru • **Angélica Escobar Chávez**, Universidad de León, Mexico • **John Fieldeldy**, College of Engineering, Nihon University, Aizuwakamatsu-shi, Japan • **Herlinda Flores**, Centro de Idiomas Universidad Veracruzana, Mexico • **Claudia Franco**, Universidad Pedagógica Nacional, Colombia • **Andrea Fredricks**, Embassy CES, San Francisco, USA • **Chen-Chen Fu**, National

Kaoshiung First Science Technology University, Taiwan • **María Irma Gallegos Peláez**, Universidad del Valle de México, Mexico City, Mexico • **Carolina García Carbajal**, El Cultural Arequipa, Peru • **Claudia Gavancho Terrazas**, ICPNA Cusco, Peru • **Adriana Gómez**, Centro Colombo Americano, Bogotá, Colombia • **Raphaël Goossens**, ICPNA Cusco, Peru • **Carlo Granados**, Universidad Central, Bogotá, Colombia • **Ralph Grayson**, Idiomas Católica, Lima, Peru • **Murat Gultekin**, Fatih University, Turkey • **Monika Hennessey**, ICPNA Chiclayo, Peru • **Lidia Hernández Medina**, Universidad del Valle de México, Mexico City, Mexico • **Jesse Huang**, National Central University, Taiwan • **Eric Charles Jones**, Seoul University of Technology, South Korea • **Jun-Chen Kuo**, Tajen University, Taiwan • **Susan Krieger**, Embassy CES, San Francisco, USA • **Robert Labelle**, Centre for Training and Development, Dawson College, Canada • **Erin Lemaistre**, Chung-Ang University, South Korea • **Eleanor S. Leu**, Soochow University, Taiwan • **Yihui Li (Stella Li)**, Fooyin University, Taiwan • **Chin-Fan Lin**, Shih Hsin University, Taiwan • **Linda Lin**, Tatung Institute of Technology, Taiwan • **Kristen Lindblom**, Embassy CES, San Francisco, USA • **Ricardo López**, PROULEX, Guadalajara, Mexico • **Neil Macleod**, Kansai Gaidai University, Osaka, Japan • **Robyn McMurray**, Pusan National University, South Korea • **Paula Medina**, London Language Institute, Canada • **María Teresa Meléndez de Elorreaga**, ICPNA Chiclayo, Peru • **Sandra Cecilia Mora Espejo**, Universidad del Valle de México, Campus Tlalpan, Mexico City, Mexico •

Ricardo Nausa, Centro Colombo Americano, Bogotá, Colombia • **Tim Newfields**, Tokyo University Faculty of Economics, Tokyo, Japan • **Mónica Nomberto**, ICPNA Chiclayo, Peru • **Scarlett Ostojic**, Idiomas Católica, Lima, Peru • **Ana Cristina Ochoa**, CCBEU Inter Americano, Curitiba, Brazil • **Doralba Pérez**, Universidad Pedagógica Nacional, Bogotá, Colombia • **David Perez Montalvo**, ICPNA Cusco, Peru • **Wahrena Elizabeth Pfeister**, University of Suwon, South Korea • **Wayne Allen Pfeister**, University of Suwon, South Korea • **Cecilia Ponce de León**, ICPNA Cusco, Peru • **Andrea Rebonato**, CCBEU Inter Americano, Curitiba, Brazil • **Elizabeth Rodríguez López**, El Cultural Trujillo, Peru • **Olga Rodríguez Romero**, El Cultural Trujillo, Peru • **Timothy Samuelson**, BridgeEnglish, Denver, USA • **Enrique Sánchez Guzmán**, PROULEX, Guadalajara, Mexico • **Letícia Santos**, ICBEU Ibiá, Brazil • **Lyndsay Shaeffer**, Embassy CES, San Francisco, USA • **John Eric Sherman**, Hong Ik University, South Korea • **João Vitor Soares**, NACC, São Paulo, Brazil • **Elena Sudakova**, English Language Center, Kiev, Ukraine • **Richard Swingle**, Kansai Gaidai College, Osaka, Japan • **Sandrine Ting**, St. John's University, Taiwan • **Shu-Ping Tsai**, Fooyin University, Taiwan • **José Luis Urbina Hurtado**, Universidad de León, Mexico • **Monica Urteaga**, Idiomas Católica, Lima, Peru • **Juan Carlos Villafuerte**, ICPNA Cusco, Peru • **Dr. Wen-hsien Yang**, National Kaohsiung Hospitality College, Kaohsiung, Taiwan • **Holger Zamora**, ICPNA Cusco, Peru.

Learning Objectives

Top Notch Fundamentals is designed for true beginning students or for students needing the support of a very low-level beginning course. No prior knowledge of English is assumed or necessary.

Unit	Communication Goals	Vocabulary	Grammar

1
Names and Occupations
page 4
	• Tell a classmate your occupation
	• Identify your classmates
	• Spell names
		• Occupations
		• The alphabet
		
		VOCABULARY BOOSTER
		
		• More occupations
			• Verb <u>be</u>:
			  ○ Singular and plural statements, contractions
			  ○ <u>Yes</u> / <u>no</u> questions and short answers
			  ○ Common errors
			• Subject pronouns
			• Articles <u>a</u> / <u>an</u>
			• Nouns:
			  ○ Singular and plural / Common and proper
			
			GRAMMAR BOOSTER • Extra practice

2 **About People** page 12	• Introduce people • Tell someone your first and last name • Get someone's contact information	• Relationships (non-family) • Titles • First and last names • Numbers 0–20 **VOCABULARY BOOSTER** • More relationships	• Possessive nouns and adjectives • <u>Be from</u> / Questions with <u>Where</u>, common errors • Verb <u>be</u>: information questions with <u>What</u> **GRAMMAR BOOSTER** • Extra practice
3 **Places and How to Get There** page 20	• Talk about locations • Discuss how to get places • Discuss transportation	• Places in the neighborhood • Locations • Ways to get places • Means of transportation • Destinations **VOCABULARY BOOSTER** • More places	• Verb <u>be</u>: questions with <u>Where</u> • Subject pronoun <u>it</u> • The imperative • <u>By</u> to express means of transportation **GRAMMAR BOOSTER** • Extra practice

4
Family
page 28
	• Identify people in your family
	• Describe your relatives
	• Talk about your family
		• Family relationships
		• Adjectives to describe people
		• Numbers 21–101
		
		VOCABULARY BOOSTER
		
		• More adjectives
			• Verb <u>be</u>:
			  ○ Questions with <u>Who</u> and common errors
			  ○ With adjectives
			  ○ Questions with <u>How old</u>
			• Adverbs <u>very</u> and <u>so</u>
			• Verb <u>have</u> / <u>has</u>: affirmative statements
			
			GRAMMAR BOOSTER • Extra practice

5 **Events and Times** page 36	• Confirm that you're on time • Talk about the time of an event • Ask about birthdays	• What time is it? • <u>Early</u>, <u>on time</u>, <u>late</u> • Events • Days of the week • Ordinal numbers • Months of the year **VOCABULARY BOOSTER** • More events	• Verb <u>be</u>: questions about time • Prepositions <u>in</u>, <u>on</u>, and <u>at</u> for dates and times • Common errors **GRAMMAR BOOSTER** • Extra practice

6
Clothes
page 44
	• Give and accept a compliment
	• Ask for colors and sizes
	• Describe clothes
		• Clothes
		• Colors and sizes
		• Opposite adjectives to describe clothes
		
		VOCABULARY BOOSTER
		
		• More clothes
			• Demonstratives <u>this</u>, <u>that</u>, <u>these</u>, <u>those</u>
			• The simple present tense: <u>like</u>, <u>want</u>, <u>need</u>, and <u>have</u>:
			  ○ Affirmative and negative statements
			  ○ Questions and short answers
			  ○ Spelling rules and contractions
			• Adjective placement and common errors
			• <u>One</u> and <u>ones</u>
			
			GRAMMAR BOOSTER • Extra practice

7
Activities
page 52
 	
Units 1-7 Review
page 60
	• Talk about morning and evening activities
	• Describe what you do in your free time
	• Discuss household chores
		• Daily activities at home
		• Leisure activities
		• Household chores
		
		VOCABULARY BOOSTER
		
		• More household chores
			• The simple present tense:
			  ○ Third-person singular spelling rules
			  ○ Questions with <u>When</u> and <u>What time</u>
			  ○ Questions with <u>How often</u>, time expressions
			  ○ Questions with <u>Who</u> as subject, common errors
			• Frequency adverbs and time expressions:
			  ○ Usage, placement, and common errors
			
			GRAMMAR BOOSTER • Extra practice

Conversation Strategies	Listening / Pronunciation	Reading / Writing
• Use <u>And you?</u> to show interest in another person • Use <u>Excuse me</u> to initiate a conversation • Use <u>Excuse me?</u> to indicate you haven't heard or didn't understand • Use <u>Thanks!</u> to acknowledge someone's complying with a request	**Listening task:** • Circle the letter you hear • Identify correct spelling of names • Write the name you hear spelled • Identify the correct occupation • Write the missing information: names and occupations **Pronunciation:** • Syllables	**Reading Text:** • Simple forms and business cards **Writing Task:** • Write affirmative and negative statements about people in a picture
• Identify someone's relationship to you when making an introduction • Use <u>too</u> to reciprocate a greeting • Begin a question with <u>And</u> to indicate you want additional information • Repeat part of a question to clarify • Repeat information to confirm	**Listening task:** • Complete statements about relationships • Circle the correct information • Fill in names, phone numbers, and e-mail addresses you hear **Pronunciation:** • Stress in two-word pairs	**Reading Text:** • Short descriptions of famous people, their occupations, and countries of origin **Writing Task:** • Write sentences about your relationships
• Use <u>You're welcome</u> to formally acknowledge thanks • Use <u>OK</u> to acknowledge advice • Use <u>What about you?</u> to show interest in another person	**Listening task:** • Write the places you hear • Write the directions you hear, using affirmative and negative imperatives • Circle the means of transportation • Write <u>by</u> phrases, check destinations you hear **Pronunciation:** • Falling intonation for questions with <u>Where</u>	**Reading Texts:** • Simple maps and diagrams • Introductions of people, their relationships and occupations, where they live, and how they get to work **Writing Task:** • Write questions and answers about the places in a complex picture
• Use <u>Well,…</u> to indicate one is deciding how to begin a response • Use <u>And how about…?</u> to ask for more information • Use <u>Really?</u> to show interest or mild surprise	**Listening task:** • Identify the picture of a relative being described • Choose the adjective that describes the people mentioned in a conversation **Pronunciation:** • Number contrasts	**Reading Texts:** • A family tree • A magazine article about famous actors and their families **Writing Task:** • Write a description of the people in your family
• Use <u>Uh-oh</u> to indicate you may have made a mistake • Use <u>Look</u> to focus someone's attention on something • Use <u>Great!</u> to show enthusiasm for an idea • Offer someone best wishes on his or her birthday	**Listening task:** • Identify events and circle the correct times • Write the events you hear in a date book • Circle the dates you hear **Pronunciation:** • Sentence rhythm	**Reading Texts:** • A world map with time zones • Events posters • Conversations • A zodiac calendar **Writing Task:** • Write about events at your school or in your city
• Acknowledge a compliment with <u>Thank you</u> • Apologize with <u>I'm sorry</u> when expressing disappointing information • Use <u>That's too bad</u> to express disappointment • Use <u>What about you?</u> to ask for someone's opinion • Use <u>Well</u> to soften a strong opinion	**Listening task:** • Confirm details about clothes • Determine colors of garments **Pronunciation:** • Plural endings	**Reading Text:** • A sales flyer from a department store **Writing Task:** • Write sentences about the clothes you have, need, want, and like
• Say <u>Me?</u> to give yourself time to think of a personal response • Use <u>Well</u> to introduce a lengthy response • Use <u>So</u> to introduce a conversation topic • Use <u>How about you?</u> to ask for parallel information • Say <u>Sure</u> to indicate a willingness to answer • Begin a response to an unexpected question with <u>Oh</u>	**Listening task:** • Match chores to the people who performed them **Pronunciation:** • Third-person singular verb endings	**Reading Text:** • A review of housekeeping robots **Writing Tasks:** • Write five sentences about robots • Describe your typical week, using adverbs of frequency and time expressions

Conversation Strategies	Listening / Pronunciation	Reading / Writing
• Use <u>Really?</u> to introduce contradictory information • Respond positively to a description with <u>Sounds nice!</u> • Use <u>Actually</u> to introduce an opinion that might surprise • Say <u>I don't know. I'm not sure</u> to avoid making a direct negative statement	**Listening task:** • Determine the best house or apartment for clients of a real estate company • Complete statements about locations of furniture and appliances **Pronunciation:** • Linking sounds	**Reading Texts:** • House and apartment rental listings • Descriptions of people and their homes **Writing Task:** • Compare and contrast your home with homes in a complex illustration
• Use <u>Hi</u> and <u>Hey</u> to greet people informally • Say <u>No kidding!</u> to show surprise • Answer the phone with <u>Hello?</u> • Identify yourself with <u>This is __</u> on the phone • Use <u>Well, actually</u> to begin an excuse • Say <u>Oh, I'm sorry</u> after interrupting • Say <u>Talk to you later</u> to indicate the end of a phone conversation	**Listening task:** • Determine weather and temperatures in cities in a weather report • Complete statements about people's activities, using the present continuous **Pronunciation:** • Rising and falling intonation of <u>yes</u> / <u>no</u> and information questions	**Reading Texts:** • A daily planner • A newspaper column about activities in a town **Writing Task:** • Write about plans for the week, using the present continuous
• Say <u>I'll check</u> to indicate you'll get information for someone • Decline an offer politely with <u>No, thanks</u> • Use <u>Please pass the ...</u> to ask for something at the table • Say <u>Here you go</u> as you offer something • Say <u>Nice to see you</u> to greet someone you already know • Use <u>You too</u> to repeat a greeting politely	**Listening task:** • Identify the foods discussed in conversations **Pronunciation:** • Vowel sounds: /i/, /ɪ/, /eɪ/, /ɛ/, /æ/	**Reading Texts:** • Recipe cards • A weekly schedule **Writing Task:** • Write about what you eat in a typical day
• Ask <u>why?</u> to ask for a clearer explanation • Use <u>What about __?</u> to ask for more information • Use <u>just</u> to minimize the importance of an action • Use a double question to clarify • Say <u>Let me think</u> to gain time to answer • Say <u>Oh yeah</u> to indicate you just remembered something	**Listening task:** • Circle the year you hear • Infer the correct day or month • Choose activities mentioned in conversations **Pronunciation:** • Simple past tense regular verb endings	**Reading Text:** • A blog in which people describe what they did the previous weekend **Writing Tasks:** • Write about the activities of two people, based on a complex picture • Write about your weekend and what you did
• Use <u>Oh</u> to indicate you've understood • Say <u>I'm sorry to hear that</u>, <u>Oh, no</u>, and <u>That's too bad</u> to express sympathy • Use <u>What's wrong?</u> to ask about an illness • Use <u>really</u> to intensify advice with <u>should</u> • Respond to good advice with <u>Good idea</u> • Say <u>I hope you feel better</u> when someone feels sick	**Listening task:** • Identify the people described in conversations • Complete statements about injuries • Identify the ailments and remedies suggested in conversations **Pronunciation** • More vowel sounds	**Reading Text:** • A magazine article about two celebrities **Writing Task:** • Write a description of someone you know
• Use <u>I wish I could . . .</u> to express a wish • Use <u>But</u> to introduce contrasting information • Suggest a shared course of action with <u>Let's</u> • Politely decline a suggestion with <u>I'm really sorry but</u> and a reason • Accept a refusal with <u>Maybe some other time</u> • Use <u>Sure</u> and <u>No problem</u> to agree to someone's request for a favor	**Listening task:** • Complete requests for favors **Pronunciation** • Assimilation of sounds: <u>Could you</u>	**Reading Text:** • A journal article about infant-toddler development **Writing Task:** • Describe things people can and can't do when they get old
• Use <u>Not really</u> to soften a negative response • Ask <u>What do you mean?</u> to request clarification • Use <u>Well</u> to explain or clarify • Use emphatic stress on <u>and</u> to indicate two answers	**Listening task:** • Choose correct statements • Circle correct words or phrases • Complete statements about activities, using the present continuous • Infer people's wishes for the future and complete statements, using <u>would like</u> **Pronunciation** • Diphthongs	**Reading Text:** • A short biography of Harry Houdini **Writing Task:** • Write your own illustrated life story, including plans and wishes for the future

What is *Top Notch*?

Top Notch is a six-level* communicative course that prepares adults and young adults to interact successfully and confidently with both native and non-native speakers of English.

The goal of the *Top Notch* course is to make English unforgettable through:

► Multiple exposures to new language
► Numerous opportunities to practice it
► Deliberate and intensive recycling

The *Top Notch* course has two beginning levels: *Top Notch* Fundamentals for true beginners and *Top Notch* 1 for false beginners.

Each full level of *Top Notch* contains enough material for 60 to 90 hours of classroom instruction. A wide choice of supplementary components makes it easy to tailor *Top Notch* to the needs of your classes.

*Summit 1 and Summit 2 are the titles of the fifth and sixth levels of the *Top Notch* course. All Student's Books are available in split editions with bound-in workbooks.

The *Top Notch* instructional design

Daily confirmation of progress

Each easy-to-follow two-page lesson begins with a clearly stated communication goal. All lesson activities are integrated with the goal and systematically build toward a final speaking activity in which students demonstrate achievement of the goal. "Can-do" statements in each unit ensure students' awareness of the continuum of their progress.

A purposeful conversation syllabus

Memorable conversation models provide essential and practical social language that students can carry "in their pockets" for use in real life. Guided conversation pair work enables students to modify, personalize, and extend each model so they can use it to communicate their own thoughts and needs. Free discussion activities are carefully crafted so students can continually retrieve and use the language from the models. All conversation models are informed by the Longman Corpus of Spoken American English.

An emphasis on cultural fluency

Recognizing that English is a global language, *Top Notch* actively equips students to interact socially with people from a variety of cultures and deliberately prepares them to understand accented speakers from diverse language backgrounds.

Intensive vocabulary development

Students actively work with a rich vocabulary of high-frequency words, collocations, and expressions in all units of the Student's Book. Clear illustrations and definitions clarify meaning and provide support for independent study, review, and test preparation. Systematic recycling promotes smooth and continued acquisition of vocabulary from the beginning to the advanced levels of the course.

A dynamic approach to grammar

An explicit grammar syllabus is supported by charts containing clear grammar rules, relevant examples, and explanations of meaning and use. Numerous grammar exercises provide focused practice, and grammar usage is continually activated in communication exercises that illustrate the grammar being learned.

A dedicated pronunciation syllabus

Focused pronunciation, rhythm, and intonation practice is included in each unit, providing application of each pronunciation point to the target language of the unit and facilitating comprehensible pronunciation.

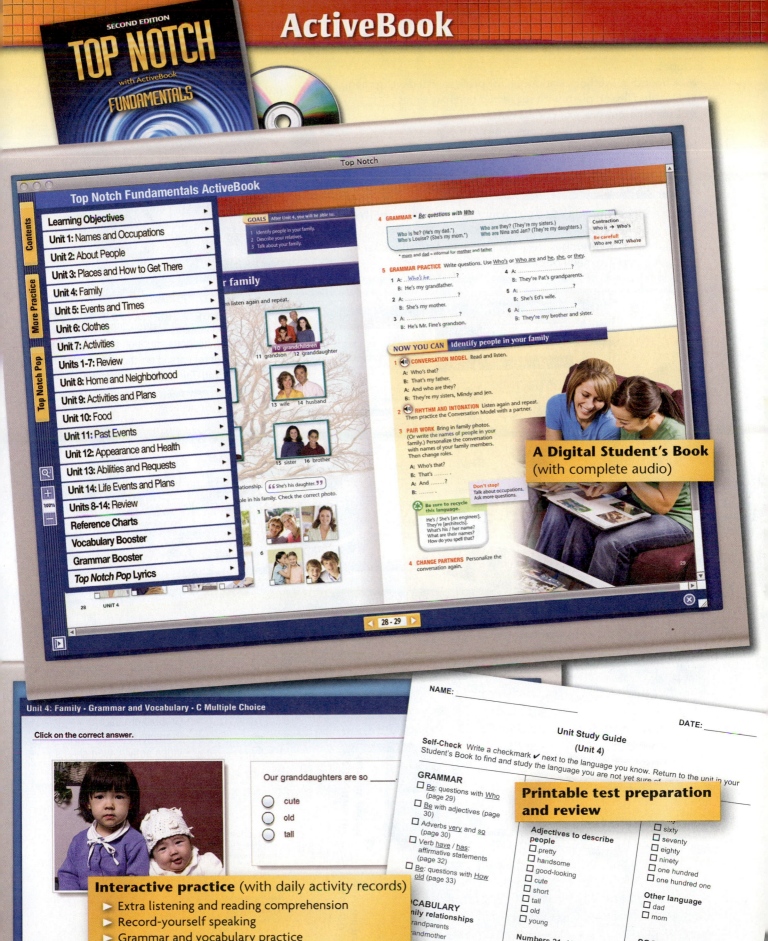

ActiveBook

SECOND EDITION
TOP NOTCH
with ActiveBook
FUNDAMENTALS

A Digital Student's Book
(with complete audio)

Printable test preparation and review

Interactive practice (with daily activity records)
► Extra listening and reading comprehension
► Record-yourself speaking
► Grammar and vocabulary practice
► Games and puzzles
► *Top Notch Pop* and karaoke

ix

The Teacher's Edition and Lesson Planner

Includes:

▶ A bound-in Methods Handbook for professional development
▶ Detailed lesson plans with suggested teaching times
▶ Language, culture, and corpus notes
▶ Student's Book and Workbook answer keys
▶ Audioscripts
▶ *Top Notch TV* teaching notes

▶ ActiveTeach

▶ A Digital Student's Book with interactive whiteboard (IWB) software
▶ Instantly accessible audio and *Top Notch TV* video
▶ Interactive exercises from the Student's *ActiveBook* for in-class use
▶ A complete menu of printable extension activities

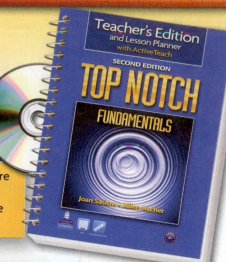

Teacher's Edition and Lesson Planner with ActiveTeach
SECOND EDITION
TOP NOTCH
FUNDAMENTALS
Joan Saslow • Allen Ascher

Top Notch TV

A hilarious situation comedy, authentic unrehearsed on-the-street interviews, and *Top Notch Pop* karaoke.

The Digital Student's Book
With zoom, write, highlight, save and other IWB tools.

Printable Extension Activities

Including:
• Writing process worksheets
• Vocabulary flashcards
• Learning strategies
• Graphic organizers
• Pronunciation activities
• Video activity worksheets and more . . .

NAME: _____ DATE: _____

Writing Process Worksheet

(Accompanies Unit 6, page 51)

ASSIGNMENT: Write about clothes you need, you want, you like, and clothes you have or don't have.

1. PREWRITING

Think about your clothes. Then fill in the chart.

What are the clothes you . . .

need?	want?	like?	have?	don't have?
white blouse	red shoes	loose clothes	old clothes	expensive clothes

2. WRITING

Write about clothes you need, you want, you like, and clothes you have or don't have. Use the information from Step 1. Add more information if you can.

For example:
I need a new white blouse. My old blouse is a little tight. I want red shoes and a ...
skirt...

They are _____.

Adjectives to describe people

The baby is _____.

Adjectives to describe people

NAME: _____

Learning Strategy

(Unit 7, page 58, Reading)

READING STRATEGY: taking notes

Take notes about key details to help you understand a reading.

PRACTICE

As you read the article on page 58, use the simple present to write what each robot does or doesn't do.

The iRobot Roomba	cleans the house
The iRobot Scooba	
ASIMO	
The L200 Evolution	

Top Notch ActiveBook CD-ROM

For Windows:

- Insert the **Top Notch ActiveBook** disc into the CD-ROM drive of your computer. On most computers, the ActiveBook menu will open automatically.

  If *ActiveBook* does not begin automatically:
- Open "**My Computer**."
- Right-click on the TN_F_ActiveBook icon. Click on **Open**.
- Double-click on the TN_F_ActiveBook.exe file to start the application. Do not remove the CD-ROM from the CD-ROM drive while using ActiveBook.
- On the opening screen, click on the book image to start ActiveBook.

For MAC:

- Insert the **Top Notch ActiveBook** disc into the CD-ROM drive of your computer.
- Double-click on the TN_F_ActiveBook icon on your desktop.
- Double click on the TN_F_ActiveBook launch file. Do not remove the CD-ROM from the CD-ROM drive while using ActiveBook.
- On the opening screen, click on the book image to start ActiveBook.

Note: The original *Top Notch ActiveBook* disc must be in the CD-ROM drive when you use this application. This application cannot be copied or used without the original CD-ROM.

ActiveBook System Requirements

	For PC-Compatible Computers	**For Macintosh Computers**
Operating System	Microsoft Windows® XP, Vista, Windows 7	Mac OSX v. 10.4.x
Processor	Intel Pentium® IV 1000MHz or faster processor (or equivalent)	PowerPC & Intel processor 500MHz or faster processor (or equivalent)
RAM	512 MB RAM minimum or higher	512 MB RAM minimum or higher
Internet Browser	Microsoft Internet Explorer® 7.x or Mozilla Firefox™ 4.x, or higher	Safari® 3.x, Mozilla Firefox™ 4.x, or higher
Plug-ins	Adobe PDF 8	Adobe PDF 8
Hardware	Computer CD-ROM drive, Sound card and speakers or headphones.	Computer CD-ROM drive, Sound card and speakers or headphones.
Monitor Resolution	1024x768	1024x768

TOP NOTCH
FUNDAMENTALS

A proven pedagogy with demonstrated results

The six-level *Top Notch* program makes English unforgettable through multiple exposures to language, numerous opportunities to practice it, and systematic and intensive recycling. Goals- and achievement-based lessons with can-do statements enable students to confirm their progress.

The leader in global communication

Top Notch prepares students to communicate in English with a diverse array of speakers around the world who have a wide range of native and non-native accents. An emphasis on cultural fluency enables students to navigate the social, travel, and business situations that they will encounter in their lives.

ActiveBook

- Student's Book in digital format with full audio
- Interactive speaking, listening, reading, grammar, and vocabulary practice
- Printable unit study guides

MyTopNotchLab

An online learning tool for personalized practice and assessment, with automatic grade book and *Top Notch TV*.

Complete and flexible

- Student's Book with ActiveBook
- Student's Book with ActiveBook and MyTopNotchLab
- Workbook
- Teacher's Edition and Lesson Planner with ActiveTeach
- Classroom Audio Program
- Copy & Go (photocopiable interactive activities)
- Complete Assessment Package
- Full-Course Placement Tests

Be a part of it: Join the Top Notch Teacher Community
www.pearsonlongman.com/topnotch2e

GSE		10	20	30	40	50	60	70	80	90
Level 3										
Level 2										
Level 1										
Fundamentals										
CEFR		<A1	A1	A2 +	B1 +	B2 +		C1	C2	

Learn about the Global Scale of English at www.englishscale.com

ISBN-13: 978-0-13-246988-3
ISBN-10: 0-13-246988-X

9 780132 469883

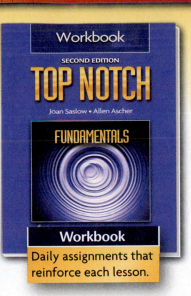

Workbook

Daily assignments that reinforce each lesson.

Classroom Audio Program

Includes a variety of authentic regional and non-native accents.

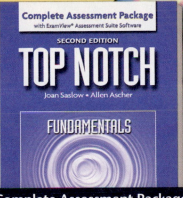

Complete Assessment Package

Ready-made achievement tests. Software provides option to edit, delete, or add items.

Full-Course Placement Tests

Choose printable or online version.

Copy & Go

Board games, role plays, information gaps, and "find someone who. . ." for every lesson.

MyTopNotchLab

An optional online learning tool with:

► An interactive *Top Notch* Workbook
► Speaking and writing activities
► Pop-up grammar help
► Student's Book *Grammar Booster* exercises
► *Top Notch TV* with extensive viewing activities
► Automatically-graded achievement tests
► Easy course management and record-keeping

Welcome to *Top Notch*!

1 🔊 **CONVERSATION MODEL** Read and listen.

1:02

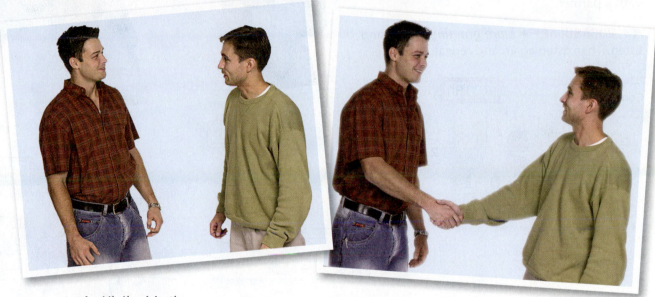

A: Hi. I'm Martin.
B: Hi, Martin. I'm Ben.

A: Nice to meet you, Ben.
B: Nice to meet you, too.

2 🔊 **RHYTHM AND INTONATION** Listen again and repeat. Then practice the Conversation Model with a partner.

1:03

NOW YOU CAN | **Introduce yourself**

PAIR WORK Now introduce yourself to your classmates.

1:04
🔊 **Greetings**
Hi.
Hello.
I'm [Lisa].

1:05
🔊 **Responses**
Nice to meet you.
Glad to meet you.
It's a pleasure to meet you.

1

GOAL   Greet people

1 🔊 **CONVERSATION MODEL** Read and listen.

1:06

A: Hi, Len. How are you?

B: Fine, thanks. And you?

A: I'm fine.

2 🔊 **RHYTHM AND INTONATION** Listen again and repeat. Then practice the Conversation Model with a partner.

1:07

3 🔊 **VOCABULARY • *More greetings*** Read and listen. Then listen again and repeat.

1:08

1 Good morning. 8:00 A.M.

2 Good afternoon. 2:00 P.M.

3 Good evening. 6:00 P.M.

NOW YOU CAN   Greet people

PAIR WORK Now greet your classmates.

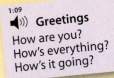

🔊 **Greetings**

1:09

How are you?
How's everything?
How's it going?

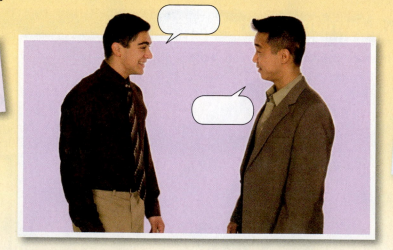

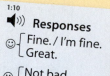

🔊 **Responses**

1:10

☺ { Fine. / I'm fine.
    Great.

☺ { Not bad.
    So-so.

Say good-bye

1 🔊 1:11 **CONVERSATION MODEL** Read and listen.

A: Good-bye, Charlotte.

B: Good-bye, Emily.

A: See you tomorrow.

B: OK. See you!

2 🔊 1:12 **RHYTHM AND INTONATION** Listen again and repeat. Then practice the Conversation Model with a partner.

NOW YOU CAN **Say good-bye**

PAIR WORK Now say good-bye to your classmates.

🔊 1:13 **Ways to say good-bye**
Good-bye.
Bye.
See you later.
Take care.

NOW I CAN... ✔

☐ Introduce myself.
☐ Greet people.
☐ Say good-bye.

Names and Occupations

GOALS After Unit 1, you will be able to:
1 Tell a classmate your occupation.
2 Identify your classmates.
3 Spell names.

LESSON 1

| GOAL | Tell a classmate your occupation |

1 1:14 🔊 **VOCABULARY** • *Occupations* Read and listen. Then listen again and repeat.

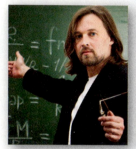

1 a teacher

2 a student

3 an architect

4 an actor

5 an athlete

6 a musician

7 an artist

8 a banker

9 a singer

10 a flight attendant

VOCABULARY BOOSTER
More occupations • p. 126

2 **PAIR WORK** Say the name of an occupation. Your partner points (☞) to the picture.

3 **GRAMMAR** • *Verb <u>be</u>: singular statements / Contractions*

Articles <u>a</u> / <u>an</u>
a teacher
an actor

Affirmative statements / Contractions

I **am** Ann. / I**'m** Ann.

You **are** an architect. / You**'re** an architect.

He **is** a teacher. / He**'s** a teacher.
She **is** a singer. / She**'s** a singer.

Negative statements / Contractions

I **am not** Jen. / I**'m not** Jen.

You **are not** an artist. / You**'re not** an artist. / You **aren't** an artist.

He **is not** a student. / He**'s not** a student. / He **isn't** a student.
She **is not** a banker. / She**'s not** a banker. / She **isn't** a banker.

4 GRAMMAR PRACTICE Write the article <u>a</u> or <u>an</u> for each occupation.

1 .... architect   3 .... banker   5 .... singer
2 .... student   4 .... musician   6 .... athlete

5 PAIR WORK Point to the people on page 4. Say *He's* __ or *She's* __ .

> " He's a teacher. "
>
> " She's a flight attendant. "

6 INTEGRATED PRACTICE Read the names and occupations. Write affirmative and negative statements.

Matt Damon
actor

CARLOS **VIVES**
SINGER

Hee-Young Lim
musician

Constantina **TOMESCU**
ATHLETE

1 Matt Damon *He's an actor. He's not an architect.*
2 Carlos Vives ....
3 Hee-Young Lim ....
4 Constantina Tomescu ....

NOW YOU CAN | **Tell a classmate your occupation**

1 🔊 **CONVERSATION MODEL** Read and listen.
1:15

A: What do you do?
B: I'm an architect. And you?
A: I'm a banker.

2 🔊 **RHYTHM AND INTONATION** Listen
1:16
again and repeat. Then practice the
Conversation Model with a partner.

3 PAIR WORK Personalize the
conversation. Use your own
occupations.

A: What do you do?
B: I'm .... And you?
A: I'm ....

4 CHANGE PARTNERS Tell another
classmate your occupation.

GOAL Identify your classmates

1 🔊 **VOCABULARY** • *More occupations* Read and listen. Then listen again and repeat.

1 She's **a chef**.

2 He's **a writer**.

3 She's **a manager**.

4 She's **a scientist**.

5 He's **a doctor**.

6 She's **an engineer**.

7 He's **a photographer**.

8 He's **a pilot**.

2 **GRAMMAR** • *Singular and plural nouns / <u>Be</u>: plural statements*

Singular nouns	Plural nouns
a chef	2 chef**s**
an athlete	3 athlete**s**

Subject pronouns

Singular	Plural
I	we
you	you
he	they
she	

Affirmative statements / Contractions
We **are** photographers. / We**'re** photographers.
You **are** scientists. / You**'re** scientists.
They **are** writers. / They**'re** writers.

Negative statements / Contractions
We **are not** chefs. / We**'re not** chefs. / We **aren't** chefs.
You **are not** pilots. / You**'re not** pilots. / You **aren't** pilots.
They **are not** artists. / They**'re not** artists. / They **aren't** artists.

3 **GRAMMAR PRACTICE** Complete each statement with a singular or plural form of <u>be</u>.

1 I .... a writer.
2 She .... not a pilot.
3 We .... doctors.
4 They .... not scientists.
5 We .... managers.

4 **INTEGRATED PRACTICE** Ⓒircle the correct word or words to complete each statement.

1 I am (an artist / artists / artist).
2 We are (a flight attendant / flight attendants / flight attendant).
3 She is (banker / a banker / bankers).
4 They are (a writer / writers / writer).

5 GRAMMAR • *Be: yes / no* questions and short answers

Yes / no questions	Short answers	
Are you / **Is he** / **Is Tanya** ⎤ an architect?	Yes, **I am.** / Yes, ⎰ he ⎱ **is.** / ⎰ she ⎱	No, **I'm not.** / No, ⎰ he's ⎱ **not.** / ⎰ she's ⎱
Are you / **Are they** / **Are Ted and Jane** ⎤ musicians?	Yes, ⎰ we ⎱ **are.** / ⎰ they ⎱	No, ⎰ we're ⎱ **not.** / ⎰ they're ⎱

Be careful!
Yes, I am. NOT ~~Yes, I'm.~~
Yes, she is. NOT ~~Yes, she's.~~
Yes, we are. NOT ~~Yes, we're.~~

6 GRAMMAR PRACTICE Complete the conversations. Use contractions when possible.

1 A: ...*Are*... they Abby and Jonah?
  B: Yes, ...

2 A: .... she Hanna?
  B: No, ... Ella.

3 A: .... you Rachel and Philip?
  B: No, we'.......... . ... Judith and Jack.

4 A: .... a chef?
  B: Yes, I ....

5 A: .... he Evan?
  B: No, ... not. He'.......... Michael.

6 A: Is .... Tim?
  B: ...., he'.......... . He's Louis.

7 PAIR WORK Practice the conversations from Exercise 6.

8 PAIR WORK Ask your partner two questions. Answer your partner's questions.

❝ Are you an artist? ❞

❝ Yes, I am. ❞

NOW YOU CAN Identify your classmates

1:18
1 ◀))) CONVERSATION MODEL Read and listen.

A: Excuse me. Are you Marie?
B: No, I'm not. I'm Laura. That's Marie.
A: Where?
B: Right over there.
A: Thank you.
B: You're welcome.

1:19
2 ◀))) RHYTHM AND INTONATION Listen again and repeat. Then practice the Conversation Model with a partner.

3 PAIR WORK Personalize the conversation. Use real names. Then change roles.

A: Excuse me. Are you ....?
B: No, I'm not. I'm .... That's ....
A: Where?
B: Right over there.
A: Thank you.
B: You're welcome.

4 CHANGE PARTNERS Identify other classmates.

GOAL | **Spell names**

1 🔊 **VOCABULARY** • *The alphabet* Read and listen. Then listen again and repeat.

ABCDEFGHIJKLM
NOPQRSTUVWXYZ

2 🔊 **LISTENING COMPREHENSION** Listen. Circle the letter you hear.

1	A K	4	U O	7	F X	10	J G	13	D G
2	B E	5	B Z	8	X S	11	L N	14	H K
3	M N	6	T C	9	Z V	12	K J	15	P E

3 **PAIR WORK** Read 10 letters aloud to your partner. Point to the letters you hear.

L W V G S
J C F I Y Q
P X B K H
R M U O N
E T A D Z

4 🔊 **LISTENING COMPREHENSION** Listen. Circle the correct spelling. Then spell each name aloud.

1	Green	Greene	Grin
2	Leigh	Lee	Li
3	Katharine	Katherine	Catharine

5 🔊 **LISTENING COMPREHENSION** Listen to the conversations. Write the names.

1 ....
2 ....
3 ....

6 **GRAMMAR** • *Proper nouns and common nouns*

> **Capital letters**
> A B C
> **Lowercase letters**
> a b c

Proper nouns
The names of people and places are proper nouns. Use a capital letter to begin a proper noun.
Melanie Pepper   New Delhi   Nicaragua

Common nouns
Other nouns are common nouns. Use a lowercase letter to begin a common noun.
morning   doctor   student

7 GRAMMAR PRACTICE Circle the proper nouns. Underline the common nouns.

1 Mary Chase   3 name   5 partners
2 letter   4 France   6 alphabet

8 GRAMMAR PRACTICE Check ☑ the common nouns. Capitalize the proper nouns.

☐ 1 marie   ☐ 3 sarah browne   ☐ 5 canada   ☐ 7 letter
☑ 2 partner   ☐ 4 teacher   ☐ 6 noun   ☐ 8 grammar

1:24
9 🔊 **PRONUNCIATION** • *Syllables* Read and listen. Then listen again and repeat.

1 syllable	2 syllables	3 syllables	4 syllables
chef	bank • er	ar • chi • tect	pho • tog • ra • pher

1:25
10 🔊 **PAIR WORK** First, take turns saying each word. Write the number of syllables. Then listen to check your work.

1 teacher ....   3 vocabulary ....   5 occupation ....
2 students ....   4 alphabet ....   6 they're ....

NOW YOU CAN   Spell names

1:26
1 🔊 **CONVERSATION MODEL** Read and listen.

A: Hello. I'm John Bello.
B: Excuse me?
A: John Bello.
B: How do you spell that?
A: B-E-L-L-O.
B: Thanks!

1:27
2 🔊 **RHYTHM AND INTONATION** Listen again and repeat. Then practice the Conversation Model with a partner.

3 PAIR WORK Personalize the conversation. Use your own name. Then change roles.

A: Hello. I'm ....
B: Excuse me?
A: ....
B: How do you spell that?
A: ....
B: Thanks!

Don't stop!
Ask about occupations.   ❝ What do you do? ❞

4 CHANGE PARTNERS Personalize the conversation again.

Extension

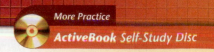

More Practice
ActiveBook *Self-Study Disc*

grammar • vocabulary • listening
reading • speaking • pronunciation

1:28
1 ◀)) **LISTENING COMPREHENSION** Listen to the conversations. Write the number of the conversation in the boxes.

1:29
2 ◀)) **LISTENING COMPREHENSION** Listen to the conversations. Complete the information.

NAME — Porter   OCCUPATION

Available for charters

John ____

PILOT

Licensed
Insured   john@airtaxi.com

World Language Institute

Lorraine Clare   1-800-555-6788

English ____

3 **PAIR WORK** Choose a famous person. Write that person's information on the form. Then play the role of that person and introduce "yourself" to your partner.

NAME:

OCCUPATION:

"Hi. I'm Sean Penn. I'm an actor. And you?"

4 **INTEGRATED PRACTICE** Answer the questions about four famous people. Use subject pronouns and contractions.

Denzel Washington
actor

Tania Libertad
singer

Se Ri Pak
athlete

Gabriel García Márquez
writer

GRAMMAR BOOSTER
Extra practice • p.136

1 Is Denzel Washington an actor or a singer?
He's an actor.

2 What's Tania Libertad's occupation?
....

3 Is Se Ri Pak a teacher?
....

4 Are Se Ri Pak and Gabriel García Márquez scientists?
....

5 What's Gabriel García Márquez's occupation?
....

6 Is Se Ri Pak an athlete?
....

5 **PERSONAL RESPONSES** Write responses with real information.

1 "Hi. I'm Art Potter."
YOU ....

2 "Are you a teacher?"
YOU ....

3 "What do you do?"
YOU ....

4 "Thank you."
YOU ....

1:30/1:31
♪ *Top Notch Pop*
"What Do You Do?"   Lyrics p. 147

R-O-S-E.

POINT Name the occupations in the pictures. For example:

She's an artist.

PAIR WORK

1 Ask and answer questions about the people. For example:

Is John a photographer? Yes, he is.

2 Create conversations for the people. For example:

Hi. I'm ___ .

WRITING Write affirmative and negative statements about the people in the picture. For example:

Rose is an artist. She's not an architect.

Rose

Ben

John

Matt

Tim

Martin

Marie

Ann

Emily

NOW I CAN... ✔

☐ Tell a classmate my occupation.
☐ Identify my classmates.
☐ Spell names.

11

About People

GOALS | After Unit 2, you will be able to:

1 Introduce people.
2 Tell someone your first and last name.
3 Get someone's contact information.

LESSON 1

GOAL | **Introduce people**

1 🔊 1:32 **VOCABULARY** • *Relationships* Read and listen. Then listen again and repeat.

1 a classmate

2 a friend

3 a neighbor

4 a boss

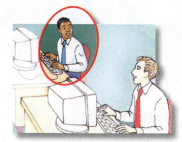

5 a colleague

VOCABULARY BOOSTER
More relationships • p. 127

2 **GRAMMAR** • *Possessive nouns and adjectives*

Possessive nouns
Al Smith is **Kate's** boss.
Larry's colleague is Teresa.
We are **Sara and Todd's** neighbors.
I am **Ms. Tan's** student.
We are **Marty's** classmates.

Possessive adjectives
He is **her** boss.
Teresa is **his** colleague.
We are **their** neighbors.
She is **my** teacher.
Marty is **our** classmate.

Ms. Ellis is **Joe's** teacher.
Joe is **her** student.

Subject pronouns		Possessive adjectives
I	→	my
you	→	your
he	→	his
she	→	her
we	→	our
they	→	their

3 **GRAMMAR PRACTICE** Circle the correct word or words to complete each sentence.

1 Mr. Thomas is (my / I) boss.
2 Is Mrs. Cory (you / your) teacher?
3 Is (she / her) Dr. Kim?
4 Are (they / their) Connie and Sam?
5 Are (your / you) Barry's friend?

6 He's (my / I) colleague.
7 Mr. Bello is (Alec / Alec's) neighbor.
8 Jake is (Ms. Rose / Ms. Rose's) student.
9 (He's / His) an architect.
10 (Kyle / Kyle's) and Ray's new classmate is Gail.

4 **PAIR WORK** Tell a classmate about at least three of your relationships. Use the Vocabulary.

❝ Jerry is my classmate. Ted and Jan Keyes are my neighbors. ❞

5 🔊 **LISTENING COMPREHENSION** Listen to the conversations. Write the relationships.

1 Bruce is her ....   **3** Mr. Grant is her ....   **5** Carlos is his ....

2 Patty is his ....   **4** Rob is her ....

6 **GRAMMAR** • *Be from* / *Questions with* *Where*

> I'm from Toronto.
>
> **Are** you **from** Paraguay?   Yes, I am. / No, I'm not.
> **Is** she **from** Moscow?   Yes, she is. / No, she's not.
>
> Where **are** you **from**?   We**'re from** Bangkok.
> Where**'s** she **from**?   She**'s from** Canada.
>
> **Be careful!** Are you from Spain?
> Yes, I am. NOT Yes, ~~I'm from~~.
>
> **Contractions**
> Where is → **Where's**
> Where are NOT ~~Where're~~

7 **GRAMMAR PRACTICE** Complete the conversations with *be from*. Use contractions when possible.

1 A: *Where's* your neighbor ....?
   B: She .... Canada.

2 A: .... they ....?
   B: .... Paris.

3 A: .... your boss ....?
   B: He .... Fortaleza.

4 A: .... you and your friend ....?
   B: .... Pusan.

NOW YOU CAN **Introduce people**

1 🔊 **CONVERSATION MODEL** Read and listen.

A: Tom, this is Paula. Paula's my classmate.

B: Hi, Paula.

C: Hi, Tom. Nice to meet you.

B: Nice to meet you, too.

2 🔊 **RHYTHM AND INTONATION** Listen again and repeat. Then practice the Conversation Model with a partner.

3 **GROUP WORK** Personalize the conversation. Introduce classmates. Use your own names. Then change roles.

A: ...., this is ....'s my ....

B: Hi, ...

C: Hi, ... Nice to meet you.

B: Nice to meet you, too.

♻ **Be sure to recycle this language.**

Don't stop! Ask questions.   Where are you from?
What do you do?

4 **CHANGE PARTNERS** Introduce other classmates.

13

GOAL | Tell someone your first and last name

1:36

1 🔊 **VOCABULARY** • *Titles and names* Read and listen. Then listen again and repeat.

Titles	👨	👩	👰	🤵
1 Mr.	✓	○	✓	○
2 Mrs.	○	○	○	✓
3 Miss	○	✓	○	○
4 Ms.	○	✓	○	✓

VOCABULARY BOOSTER
More titles • p. 127

Mr. Charles Lee   Mrs. Vivian Lee
5 first name   **6 last name**

Be careful!
Mr. Charles Lee OR Mr. Lee
Mrs. Vivian Lee OR Mrs. Lee
NOT ~~Mr. Charles~~
NOT ~~Mrs. Vivian~~

2 PAIR WORK Introduce yourself to a classmate. Use a title and your last name.

❝ Hi. I'm Mr. Wilson. ❞

❝ Nice to meet you, Mr. Wilson. ❞

1:37

3 🔊 **LISTENING COMPREHENSION** Listen. Circle the correct information. Then listen again and check your answers.

1
- ☒ Mr.
- ☐ Mrs.
- ☐ Miss
- ☐ Ms.

(Alex) Davis
first name   last name

2
- ☐ Mr.
- ☐ Mrs.
- ☐ Miss
- ☒ Ms.

Nancy Sullivan
first name   last name

3
- ☒ Mr.
- ☐ Mrs.
- ☐ Miss
- ☐ Ms.

Frank Sun
first name   last name

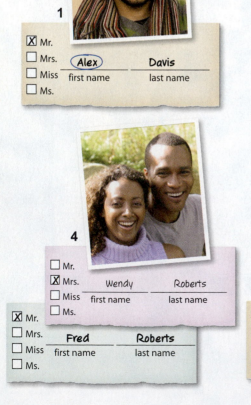

4
- ☐ Mr.
- ☒ Mrs.
- ☐ Miss
- ☐ Ms.

Wendy Roberts
first name   last name

- ☒ Mr.
- ☐ Mrs.
- ☐ Miss
- ☐ Ms.

Fred Roberts
first name   last name

5
- ☐ Mr.
- ☐ Mrs.
- ☐ Miss
- ☒ Ms.

RITA OLIVEIRA
first name   last name

6
- ☐ Mr.
- ☐ Mrs.
- ☐ Miss
- ☒ Ms.

Pam García
first name   last name

- ☒ Mr.
- ☐ Mrs.
- ☐ Miss
- ☐ Ms.

Henry Solas
first name   last name

4 VOCABULARY PRACTICE Fill out the forms. Check or circle the correct titles.

You:

☐ Mr.	☐ Mrs.	☐ Miss	☐ Ms.

_____ _____
first name   last name

A classmate:

☐ Mr.
☐ Mrs.   first name
☐ Miss
☐ Ms.
                    last name

Your teacher:

☐ Mr.   ☐ Mrs.   ☐ Miss   ☐ Ms.

_____ _____
first name   last name

NOW YOU CAN   Tell someone your first and last name

1 🔊 **CONVERSATION MODEL** Read and listen.
1:38

A: What's your last name, please?

B: Fava.

A: And your first name?

B: My first name? Bob.

A: Thank you, Mr. Fava.

B: You're welcome.

2 🔊 **RHYTHM AND INTONATION** Listen again and repeat.
1:39
Then practice the Conversation Model with a partner.

3 **PAIR WORK** Personalize the conversation. Use your own names.
Write your partner's information on the form. Then change roles.

Mr.
Mrs. _____ _____
Miss   first name   last name
Ms.

A: What's your last name, please?

B: ....

A: And your first name?

B: My first name? ....

A: Thank you, ...

B: You're welcome.

Don't stop!
Ask more questions.

♻ **Be sure to recycle this language.**

How do you spell that?
What do you do?
Where are you from?

4 **CHANGE PARTNERS** Personalize the conversation again.

15

GOAL   Get someone's contact information

1 🔊)) **VOCABULARY** • *Numbers 0 – 20* Read
and listen. Then listen again and repeat.

0 zero   7 seven   14 fourteen
1 one   8 eight   15 fifteen
2 two   9 nine   16 sixteen
3 three   10 ten   17 seventeen
4 four   11 eleven 18 eighteen
5 five   12 twelve 19 nineteen
6 six   13 thirteen 20 twenty

2 **PAIR WORK** Read a number aloud from the picture.
Your partner writes the number on a separate sheet
of paper.

3 **GRAMMAR** • *Be: information questions with What*

What's his name?   (Mark Crandall.)
What's his last name?   (Crandall.)
What's Ellen's address?   (18 Main Street.)
What's her e-mail address? (Dover14@hipnet.com.)
What's their phone number? (835-555-0037.)

What are their first names? (Luis and Samuel.)

What is → What's

**How to say e-mail addresses
  and phone numbers:**
Say "dover fourteen **at** hipnet **dot** com."
Say *"oh"* for *zero:* 0037 = *"oh-oh-three-seven."*

4 🔊)) **PRONUNCIATION** • *Stress in two-word pairs* Read and listen. Then listen again and repeat.

• •   • • •   • • •
first name   **phone** num ber   **e-mail** address

5 🔊)) **LISTENING COMPREHENSION** Listen to the conversations. Write the
information. Then listen again and check your work.

	NAME		PHONE NUMBER	E-MAIL
1	Valerie	Peterson	_ _ _ - _ _ _ _	_ _ _ _ _ _ _ @ _ _ _ _ _ _
2	Mathilda		_ _ _ - _ _ _ - _ _ _ _	
3		Quinn	_ _ _ - _ _ _ _	_ _ _ _ _ _ @ _ _ _ _ _
4	Joseph		_ _ _ - _ _ - _ _ - _ _	

6 INTEGRATED PRACTICE Complete the questions.

1 A: What's his address?
B: 11 Main Street.

2 A: .... phone number?
B: 22-63-140.

3 A: .... address?
B: 18 Bank Street.

4 A: .... phone number?
B: 878-456-0055.

5 A: .... e-mail address?
B: It's sgast@mp.net.

6 A: .... phone number?
B: 44-78-35.

NOW YOU CAN Get someone's contact information

1 🔊 1:43 **CONVERSATION MODEL** Read and listen.

A: What's your name?
B: Dave Mitchell.
A: And what's your phone number?
B: 523-6620.
A: 523-6620?
B: That's right.

2 🔊 1:44 **RHYTHM AND INTONATION** Listen again and repeat.
Then practice the Conversation Model with a partner.

3 PAIR WORK Personalize the conversation. Write your
partner's answers on a separate sheet of paper.
Then change roles.

A: What's your ....?
B: ....
A: And what's your phone number?
B: ....
A: ....?
B: That's right.

Don't stop!
Continue the conversation.
Ask more questions.

 Be sure to recycle this language.

first name / last name
address / e-mail address
Thank you.
You're welcome.
Nice to meet you.
Good-bye.

4 CHANGE PARTNERS Get other classmates' contact information.

Extension

1 1:45 🔊 **READING** Read about six famous people. Where are they from?

This is Frank Gehry. Where is Mr. Gehry from? He's from Canada. And what's his occupation? He's an architect.

This is Paco de Lucía, from Spain. What's his occupation? He's a musician.

This is Maria Sharapova. She's from Russia. What's Ms. Sharapova's occupation? She's an athlete.

This is John Travolta. Mr. Travolta has two occupations. He's an actor and a pilot. He's from the United States.

This is Angélique Kidjo. What's her occupation? Ms. Kidjo is a singer. She's from Benin.

This is Banana Yoshimoto. Ms. Yoshimoto is from Japan. What's her occupation? She's a writer.

2 **PAIR WORK** Ask and answer questions about people in the Reading. Use the verb <u>be</u>.

❝ Is Frank Gehry a doctor? ❞

❝ Is Maria Sharapova from the United States? ❞

❝ Where's Mr. Travolta from? ❞

On your *ActiveBook* Self-Study Disc:
Extra Reading Comprehension Questions

3 **SPEAKING** Point to the people in the photos. Ask your partner questions about their contact information.

Ryan Hale

🏠 12 Bank St.
📧 rhale@ccc.com

Norma Chin

☎ 33-55-0078
📧 nchin@hipnet.com

Fran Green   Bill Green

☎ 34-67-9899
🏠 13 Quinn St.

GRAMMAR BOOSTER

Extra practice • p.137

🎵 1:46/1:47
Top Notch Pop
"Excuse Me, Please"   Lyrics p. 147

PERSONAL INFORMATION

First name:	Last name:
Address:	
Phone:	e-mail:

PAIR WORK

1 Create a conversation for the people in the first picture. Complete the form with your partner's information. Start like this:

What's your ___?

2 Create a conversation for the people in the second picture. Introduce the two women. Start like this:

This is ___. She's my ___.

WRITING Write sentences about your relationships. For example:

Nancy Lee is my friend. She's from Vancouver.

She's a . . .

NOW I CAN... ✔

- ☐ Introduce people.
- ☐ Tell someone my first and last name.
- ☐ Get someone's contact information.

Places and How to Get There

GOALS After Unit 3, you will be able to:

1 Talk about locations.
2 Discuss how to get places.
3 Discuss transportation.

LESSON 1

GOAL	Talk about locations

1 🔊 1:48 **VOCABULARY** • *Places in the neighborhood* Read and listen. Then listen again and repeat.

1 a pharmacy

2 a restaurant

3 a bank

4 a school

5 a newsstand

6 a bookstore

VOCABULARY BOOSTER

More places • p. 127

2 🔊 1:49 **LISTENING COMPREHENSION** Listen. Write the places you hear.

1 ....

2 ....

3 ....

4 ....

3 **PAIR WORK** Say the name of a place. Your partner writes the word.

4 🔊 1:50 **VOCABULARY** • *Locations* Read and listen. Then listen again and repeat.

1 across the street

2 down the street

3 around the corner

4 on the left

5 on the right

6 next to the bank

7 between the bookstore and the bank

5 PAIR WORK Take turns making statements about the location of the places.

" The bank is across the street. "

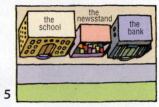

1   2   3   4   5

6 GRAMMAR • *Be: questions with Where / Subject pronoun it*

Ask questions with <u>Where</u> for locations.
Where's the restaurant?

Use <u>it</u> to replace the names of places.
It's down the street. (<u>It</u> = the restaurant)

Contractions
Where is → Where's
It is → It's

1:51

7 ◀)) **PRONUNCIATION** • *Falling intonation for questions with <u>Where</u>* Read and listen. Then listen again and repeat.

1 Where is it?

2 Where's the bank?

3 Where's the school?

4 Where's the newsstand?

NOW YOU CAN | **Talk about locations**

1:52

1 ◀)) **CONVERSATION MODEL** Read and listen.

A: Excuse me. Where's the bank?

B: The bank? It's around the corner.

A: Thanks!

B: You're welcome.

1:53

2 ◀)) **RHYTHM AND INTONATION** Listen again and repeat. Then practice the Conversation Model with a partner.

3 PAIR WORK Find the people on the map. Talk about the location of places on the map. Then change roles.

A: Excuse me. Where's the ....?

B: ....? It's ....

A: Thanks!

B: You're welcome.

4 CHANGE PARTNERS Ask about other locations.

GOAL | Discuss how to get places

1 🔊 1:54 **VOCABULARY** • *Ways to get places* Read and listen. Then listen again and repeat.

1 walk

2 drive

3 take a taxi

4 take the train

5 take the bus

2 **GRAMMAR** • *The imperative*

Use imperatives to give instructions and directions.

Affirmative imperatives	Negative imperatives
Drive [to the bank].	**Don't walk.**
Take the bus [to the pharmacy].	**Don't take** the train.

Do not → Don't

3 **INTEGRATED PRACTICE** Follow the directions.

Partner A: Read a direction.
Partner B: Say the letter of the correct picture.

1 Walk to the bookstore.
2 Don't drive to the restaurant.
3 Take the bus to the bank.
4 Don't walk to the pharmacy.
5 Drive down the street.

Partner B: Read a direction.
Partner A: Say the letter of the correct picture.

6 Take the bus down the street.
7 Don't take the bus to the bank.
8 Walk to the bank.
9 Take a taxi to the restaurant.
10 Drive to the pharmacy.

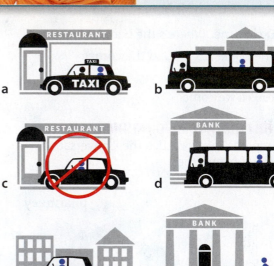

a

b

c

d

e

f

g

h

i

j

4 🔊 **LISTENING COMPREHENSION** Listen. Write the directions. Use an affirmative and a negative imperative.

1 *Take the bus. Don't drive.*   **3** ....   **5** ....

2 ....   **4** ....

NOW YOU CAN   Discuss how to get places

1 🔊 **CONVERSATION MODEL** Read and listen.

A: Can I walk to the bookstore?

B: The bookstore? Sure.

A: And what about the school?

B: The school? Don't walk. Drive.

A: OK. Thanks!

2 🔊 **RHYTHM AND INTONATION** Listen again and repeat. Then practice the Conversation Model with a partner.

3 **PAIR WORK** Change the model. Use the photos below. Ask how to get to places in the neighborhood. Then change roles.

A: Can I walk to the ....?

B: The ....? ....

A: And what about the ....?

B: The ....? Don't ....

A: OK. Thanks!

♻ **Be sure to recycle this language.**

> **Don't stop!**
> Ask about locations.

Where is it?

It's { across the street.
down the street.
around the corner.
next to the ___.
between the ___ and the ___.

4 **CHANGE PARTNERS** Discuss more places.

GOAL | Discuss transportation

1 🔊 1:58 **VOCABULARY** • *Means of transportation* Read and listen. Then listen again and repeat.

1 a car

2 a bicycle

3 a moped

4 a subway

5 a motorcycle

Also remember:
a bus
a train
a taxi

2 PAIR WORK Take turns. Spell a Vocabulary word aloud. Your partner writes the word.

3 GRAMMAR • *By to express means*

by taxi   **by** bicycle   **by** motorcycle

4 🔊 1:59 **LISTENING COMPREHENSION** Listen. Circle the means of transportation you hear.

1   2   3

4   5

5 🔊 1:60 **VOCABULARY** • *Destinations* Read and listen. Then listen again and repeat.

1 go to work

2 go home

3 go to school

6 🔊 1:61 **LISTENING COMPREHENSION** Listen. Use a <u>by</u> phrase to write the means of transportation. Then check the box for work, home, or school.

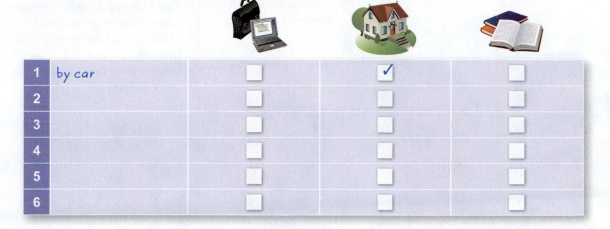

		💼	🏠	📚
1	by car	☐	✓	☐
2		☐	☐	☐
3		☐	☐	☐
4		☐	☐	☐
5		☐	☐	☐
6		☐	☐	☐

NOW YOU CAN   Discuss transportation

1 🔊 1:62 **CONVERSATION MODEL** Read and listen.

A: How do you go to school?

B: By subway. What about you?

A: Me? I walk.

2 🔊 1:63 **RHYTHM AND INTONATION** Listen again and repeat. Then practice the Conversation Model with a partner.

3 **PAIR WORK** Personalize the conversation. Ask about work, school, and home. Answer with a <u>by</u> phrase. Then change roles.

A: How do you go ....?

B: .... What about you?

A: Me? I ....

Don't stop!
Ask about other places.

4 **CHANGE PARTNERS** Personalize the conversation again.

25

Extension

1 🔊 **READING** Read about how people go to work and school.

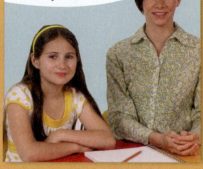

I'm Kim Lee. I'm an engineer. I'm lucky. I can walk to work. My office is around the corner from my home.

I'm Jennie Beck. I'm a writer from New York. I go to work by subway. I take the subway home, too.

I'm a doctor. My name is Jasper White. I go to work by train, and I go home by car with my colleague, Dr. Randall Marshall. He's a neighbor down the street from my home.

I'm Katie Simpson, and this is my teacher, Ms. Clark. I'm a student. My school is right next to my home. I walk to school with my friends. We walk home together, too.

I'm Hillary Clark. I'm Katie's teacher, but *my* home is not next to our school. Can I walk to school? Definitely not! I take the bus to school, and I go home by train.

2 PAIR WORK Ask and answer the questions.

On your *ActiveBook* Self-Study Disc:
Extra Reading Comprehension Questions

❝ Is Jennie Beck a teacher? ❞

❝ No, she's not. She's a writer. ❞

1 Is Jasper White a doctor?
2 Is Randall Marshall Dr. White's friend or his colleague?
3 Is Dr. Marshall Dr. White's neighbor?
4 Is Katie Simpson a teacher?
5 What is Katie's teacher's name?
6 Is their school next to Ms. Clark's home?
7 Where is Kim Lee's office?
8 Your own question: ....?

GRAMMAR BOOSTER
Extra practice • p. 138

3 GROUP WORK On the board, make a map of places near your school. Write the names of the places. Then take turns describing the locations of the places.

 Be sure to recycle this language.

Where's the [pharmacy]?	Walk / Don't [drive].
It's ___.	Go by bus.
Can I [walk] to the [restaurant]?	Don't go by train.
Take / Don't take the [bus].	

CONTEST Study the picture for one minute. Then close your books. Who can remember all of the locations? For example:

The school is down the street.

PAIR WORK Create conversations for the people. For example:

A: How do you go to work?
B: By bus.

WRITING Write five questions and answers about the places in the picture. For example:

Where's the restaurant?

It's across the street.

NOW I CAN... ✔

☐ Talk about locations.
☐ Discuss how to get places.
☐ Discuss transportation.

GOALS | After Unit 4, you will be able to:

1 Identify people in your family.
2 Describe your relatives.
3 Talk about your family.

LESSON 1

GOAL | **Identify people in your family**

1 🔊 2:02 **VOCABULARY** • *Family relationships* Read and listen. Then listen again and repeat.

1 grandparents

2 grandmother

3 grandfather

10 grandchildren
11 grandson   **12** granddaughter

4 parents

5 mother

6 father

13 wife   **14** husband

7 children*

8 daughter

9 son

15 sister   **16** brother

* one **child** / two **children**

2 **PAIR WORK** Point to two people in the family. Describe their relationship. ❝She's his daughter.❞

3 🔊 2:03 **LISTENING COMPREHENSION** Listen to a man identify people in his family. Check the correct photo.

1

☐ ☐

2

☐ ☐

3

☐ ☐

4

☐ ☐

5

☐ ☐

6

☐ ☐

4 GRAMMAR • _Be_: questions with _Who_

Who is he? (He's my dad.*)
Who's Louise? (She's my mom.*)

Who are they? (They're my sisters.)
Who are Nina and Jan? (They're my daughters.)

Contraction
Who is → Who's

Be careful!
Who are NOT ~~Who're~~

* <u>mom</u> and <u>dad</u> = informal for <u>mother</u> and <u>father</u>

5 GRAMMAR PRACTICE Write questions. Use <u>Who's</u> or <u>Who are</u> and <u>he</u>, <u>she</u>, or <u>they</u>.

1 A: _Who's he_ ....?
   B: He's my grandfather.

2 A: ....?
   B: She's my mother.

3 A: ....?
   B: He's Mr. Fine's grandson.

4 A: ....?
   B: They're Pat's grandparents.

5 A: ....?
   B: She's Ed's wife.

6 A: ....?
   B: They're my brother and sister.

NOW YOU CAN Identify people in your family

2:04

1 🔊 **CONVERSATION MODEL** Read and listen.

A: Who's that?
B: That's my father.
A: And who are they?
B: They're my sisters, Mindy and Jen.

2:05

2 🔊 **RHYTHM AND INTONATION** Listen again and repeat.
Then practice the Conversation Model with a partner.

3 **PAIR WORK** Bring in family photos.
(Or write the names of people in your
family.) Personalize the conversation
with names of your family members.
Then change roles.

A: Who's that?
B: That's ....
A: And ....?
B: ....

Don't stop!
Talk about occupations.
Ask more questions.

 **Be sure to recycle
this language.**

He's / She's [an engineer].
They're [architects].
What's his / her name?
What are their names?
How do you spell that?

4 **CHANGE PARTNERS** Personalize the
conversation again.

GOAL Describe your relatives

VOCABULARY BOOSTER
More adjectives • p. 128

1 🔊 **VOCABULARY** • *Adjectives to describe people*
2:06
Read and listen. Then listen again and repeat.

1 pretty   **2** handsome

3 good-looking

4 cute   **5** short   **6** tall   **7** old   **8** young

2 **GRAMMAR** • *Be with adjectives / Adverbs very and so*

> **Describe people with a form of _be_ and an adjective.**
> She's **pretty**.   They're **good-looking**.
> He's **handsome**.   Your children **are cute**.
>
> **The adverbs _very_ and _so_ make adjectives stronger.**
> They're **very good-looking**.   She's **so pretty**!
> He's **very handsome**.   Your children are **so cute**!

3 **PAIR WORK** Use the Vocabulary to describe two people in your class.

> ❝Gina and Deborah are very pretty.❞

4 🔊 **LISTENING COMPREHENSION** Listen to the conversations.
2:07
Circle the adjective that describes each person.

1 Her husband is (handsome / tall / old).

2 His daughter is (tall / good-looking / cute).

3 Her brothers are (tall / good-looking / young).

4 His son is (tall / good-looking / short).

5 Her father is (tall / old / short).

6 His sisters are (tall / good-looking / short).

5 **INTEGRATED PRACTICE** Look at the pictures. Complete each sentence with a form of _be_ and an adjective.

1 Your sisters ....
so ....

2 Your daughter ....
so ....!

3 Our grandfather ....
very ....

4 His girlfriend .... very ....

5 His wife .... so ....!

6 Your brother .... so tall. And his colleague .... very ....

6 **INTEGRATED PRACTICE** Write three sentences about people in your family. Use adjectives and the adverbs <u>very</u> or <u>so</u> to describe the people.

> My brother is very tall.

NOW YOU CAN Describe your relatives

1 🔊 2:08 **CONVERSATION MODEL** Read and listen.

A: Tell me about your father.

B: Well, he's a doctor. And he's very tall.

A: And how about your mother?

B: She's a scientist. She's very pretty.

2 🔊 2:09 **RHYTHM AND INTONATION** Listen again and repeat. Then practice the Conversation Model with a partner.

3 **PAIR WORK** Personalize the conversation. Describe your relatives. Then change roles.

A: Tell me about your ....

B: Well, ... And ....

A: And how about your ....?

B: ....

> **Don't stop!**
> Ask about other people in your partner's family.

4 **CHANGE PARTNERS** Ask about other classmates' relatives.

31

GOAL	Talk about your family

1 GRAMMAR • Verb _have_ / _has_: affirmative statements

> I **have** one son and one daughter.

I
You
We
They } **have** a brother.   He
She } **has** three sisters.

2 GRAMMAR PRACTICE Complete the sentences. Use _have_ or _has_. Then complete the sentence about your own family.

1 Mark .... two brothers.

2 My grandmother .... five grandsons.

3 They .... a granddaughter.

4 We .... twelve grandchildren.

5 Carl and Anna .... two children.

6 She .... five sisters.

7 They .... no brothers or sisters.

YOU I ....

3 ◀)) VOCABULARY • _Numbers 21–101_ Read and listen. Then listen again and repeat.

2:10

21 twenty-one	25 twenty-five	29 twenty-nine	40 forty	80 eighty
22 twenty-two	26 twenty-six	30 thirty	50 fifty	90 ninety
23 twenty-three	27 twenty-seven	31 thirty-one	60 sixty	100 one hundred
24 twenty-four	28 twenty-eight	32 thirty-two	70 seventy	101 one hundred one

4 ◀)) PRONUNCIATION • _Numbers_ Listen and repeat. Then practice saying the numbers on your own.

2:11

13 • 30	17 • 70
14 • 40	18 • 80
15 • 50	19 • 90
16 • 60	

5 PAIR WORK Take turns saying a number from the chart. Your partner circles the number.

23	45	40	18	94	21	20	14
58	102	43	89	90	44	53	13
30	19	60	99	22	50	52	100
15	47	33	54	17	66	77	70
64	78	95	80	87	101	1	31

6 GRAMMAR • _Be_: questions with _How old_

How old are you?

I'm three.

How old is	he? she? your sister?	He's nineteen years old. She's thirty-three. She's twenty.
How old are	they? your parents?	They're twenty-nine. They're fifty and fifty-two.

7 GRAMMAR PRACTICE Complete the questions. Use _How old is_ or _How old are_.

1 .... your sister?

2 .... Matt's parents?

3 .... your grandfather?

4 .... Helen's husband?

5 .... her children?

6 .... his son?

NOW YOU CAN Talk about your family

1 ◀ᴗ)) CONVERSATION MODEL Read and listen. `2:12`

A: I have one brother and two sisters.

B: Really? How old is your brother?

A: Twenty.

B: And your sisters?

A: Eighteen and twenty-two.

2 ◀ᴗ)) RHYTHM AND INTONATION Listen again `2:13`
and repeat. Then practice the Conversation
Model with a partner.

3 PAIR WORK Personalize the conversation.
Talk about your own family. Then
change roles.

A: I have ....

B: Really? How old ....?

A: ....

B: And your ....?

A: ....

> **Don't stop!** Ask more questions.
> Tell me about your [mother].
> And your [father]?
> How about your [grandparents]?
>
> What's his / her name?
> What are their names?
>
> What's his / her occupation?
> What are their occupations?

4 CHANGE PARTNERS
Personalize the conversation again.

1 🔊 **READING** Read about some famous actors and their families and friends.

Who Are They?

This is **Jackie Chan.**
Mr. Chan is an actor and a
singer from Hong Kong.
His wife is Joan Lin. She is
an actress from Taiwan. Her
Chinese name is Lin Feng–Jiao.
They have a son, JC Chan. He's
an actor and a singer, too.

This is **Abigail Breslin.** She's an actress
from the United States. She's very young,
and she's a movie star, too. She has two
brothers, Ryan and Spencer. Spencer is also
an actor. Miss Breslin lives with her parents,
Michael and Kim Breslin, in New York. Her
grandparents, Catherine and Lynn Blecker,
say she's very cute in her movies.

This is **Gael García Bernal,** on the left,
with his good friend, **Diego Luna,** on the
right. Mr. García Bernal is a famous actor
from Mexico. His parents, Patricia Bernal
and José Ángel García, are actors, too. He
has one sister and two brothers. Mr. Luna
is also an actor. Many people think they are
both very handsome.

2 READING COMPREHENSION Read about the people again. Complete the sentences.

1 Jackie Chan is JC Chan's ....

2 .... is Lin Feng-Jiao's husband.

3 Abigail Breslin's .... is an actor.

4 Miss Breslin is Lynn Blecker's ....

5 Gael García Bernal is Diego
Luna's ....

6 Patricia Bernal, José Ángel García, and
Diego Luna are ....

On your *ActiveBook* Self-Study Disc:
Extra Reading Comprehension Questions

3 PAIR WORK Interview your partner. Complete the notepad with
information about your partner's family.

Relative's name	Relationship	Age	Occupation	Description
Doug	brother	14	student	He's very tall.

Relative's name	Relationship	Age	Occupation	Description

GRAMMAR BOOSTER
Extra practice • p. 138

4 GROUP WORK Now tell your classmates about
your partner's family.

❝ Doug is Laura's brother.
He's 14. . . . ❞

2:15/2:16
🎵 *Top Notch Pop*
"Tell Me All About It" Lyrics p. 147

PAIR WORK

1 Ask and answer questions about the people. For example:

A: Who's Meg?
B: She's Sue's mother.
A: Is Dora Meg's daughter?
B: No, she's not.

2 Take turns making statements about the family relationships. For example:

Mike has two children. Pia is his daughter.

DESCRIPTION Choose a photo. Use adjectives to describe the people in the family. For example:

Pia is very cute.

WRITING Write ten sentences to describe the people in <u>your</u> family. For example:

My grandparents are very good-looking.

NOW I CAN...

- [ ] Identify people in my family.
- [ ] Describe my relatives.
- [ ] Talk about my family.

Events and Times

GOALS   After Unit 5, you will be able to:

1 Confirm that you're on time.
2 Talk about the time of an event.
3 Ask about birthdays.

LESSON 1

GOAL **Confirm that you're on time**

1 🔊 **VOCABULARY** • *What time is it?* Read and listen. Then listen again and repeat.

2:17

1 It's one o'clock.

2 It's one fifteen.
It's a quarter after one.

3 It's one twenty.
It's twenty after one.

4 It's one thirty.
It's half past one.

5 It's one forty.
It's twenty to two.

6 It's one forty-five.
It's a quarter to two.

7 It's noon.

8 It's midnight.

24:00 ➜ 11:59 = A.M.
12:00 ➜ 23:59 = P.M.

Say "eight A.M."
or "eight P.M."

2 🔊 **PRONUNCIATION** • *Sentence rhythm* Read and listen.
Then listen again and repeat.

2:18

1 It's **TEN** after **FIVE**.   **2** It's **TWEN**ty to **ONE**.   **3** It's a **QUAR**ter to **TWO**.

3 **PRONUNCIATION PRACTICE** Read the times in the Vocabulary aloud again.
Pay attention to sentence rhythm.

4 **PAIR WORK** Look at the map. Ask your partner about times around the world. Say each time two ways.

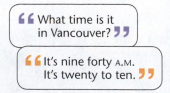

❝ What time is it in Vancouver? ❞

❝ It's nine forty A.M. It's twenty to ten. ❞

5 🔊 **VOCABULARY** • *Early, <u>on time</u>, and <u>late</u>* Read and listen. Then listen again and repeat.

1 She's **early**.

2 They're **on time**.

3 He's **late**.

NOW YOU CAN Confirm that you're on time

1 🔊 **CONVERSATION MODEL** Read and listen.

A: What time is the meeting?

B: 10:00.

A: Uh-oh. Am I late?

B: No, you're not. It's five to ten.

A: Five to ten?

B: That's right. You're early.

2 🔊 **RHYTHM AND INTONATION** Listen again and repeat. Then practice the Conversation Model with a partner.

3 PAIR WORK It's 2:15 P.M. now. Change the model. Use the pictures. Then change roles.

A: What time is the ....?

B: ....

A: Uh-oh. Am I late?

B: .... It's ....

A: ....?

B: That's right. You're ....

class: 2:15 P.M.

train: 2:30 P.M.

bus: 2:00 P.M.

4 CHANGE PARTNERS Change the model again.

GOAL **Talk about the time of an event**

VOCABULARY BOOSTER
More events • p. 128

1 2:22 🔊 **VOCABULARY** • *Events* Read and listen. Then listen again and repeat.

1 a party

2 a dance

3 a game

4 a dinner

5 a movie

6 a concert

2 2:23 🔊 **LISTENING COMPREHENSION** Listen to the conversations about events.
Write the event and circle the time.

1 .... (7:15 / 7:45)   4 .... (12:00 A.M. / 12:00 P.M.)
2 .... (8:00 / 9:00)   5 .... (9:15 / 9:50)
3 .... (3:30 / 3:15)   6 .... (12:00 A.M. / 12:00 P.M.)

3 2:24 🔊 **VOCABULARY** • *Days of the week* Read and listen. Then listen again and repeat.

WEEKDAYS					THE WEEKEND	
Monday	Tuesday	Wednesday	Thursday	Friday	Saturday	Sunday

4 **GRAMMAR** • *Be: questions about time / Prepositions at and on*

What time is it?   (It's) five twenty.
What time's the party?   (It's) **at** nine thirty.
What day is the concert?   (It's) **on** Saturday.

When's the dance?   ⎰(It's) **at** ten o'clock.
                               ⎱(It's) **on** Friday at 10:00 P.M.

Contractions
What time is → **What time's**
   When is → **When's**

Be careful!
What time is it? NOT What ~~time's~~ it?
When is it? NOT ~~When's~~ it?

5 GRAMMAR PRACTICE Complete the questions and answers.

1 A: When .... the party?
B: It's .... 11:00 P.M.

2 A: .... day is the game?
B: It's .... Saturday.

3 A: What .... is the concert?
B: It's .... 8:30.

4 A: What .... is the dinner?
B: It's .... Tuesday.

5 A: .... is the dance?
B: It's .... Friday at 9:00.

6 A: What .... is the class?
B: It's .... noon.

6 2:25 🔊 **LISTENING COMPREHENSION** Listen to the conversation. Write the events on the calendar.

Monday	5:30		**Thursday**	5:30	
	6:30			6:30	
	7:00			7:00	*meeting*
	7:15			7:15	
Tuesday	5:30		**Friday**	5:30	
	6:30			6:30	
	7:00			7:00	
	7:15			7:15	
Wednesday	5:30		**Saturday**	5:30	**Sunday** 5:30
	6:30			6:30	6:30
	7:00			7:00	7:00
	7:15			7:15	7:15

NOW YOU CAN | Talk about the time of an event

1 2:26 🔊 **CONVERSATION MODEL** Read and listen.

A: Look. There's a dance on Wednesday.
B: Great! What time?
A: 10:30. At Pat's Restaurant.
B: Really? Let's meet at 10:15.

2 2:27 🔊 **RHYTHM AND INTONATION** Listen again and repeat. Then practice the Conversation Model with a partner.

3 PAIR WORK Change the model. Ask your partner about an event. Use these events or your own events. Then change roles.

A: Look. There's a .... on ....
B: Great! What time?
A: .... At ....
B: Really? Let's meet at ....

4 CHANGE PARTNERS Talk about different events.

School Dance
WEDNESDAY, 10:30 P.M.
Pat's Restaurant

Basketball Game
Saturday 10:00 A.M.
At Athlete Central

MOVIE NIGHT
LITTLE MISS SUNSHINE
with Abigail Breslin
Thursday, 9:00 P.M.
Marcy's Books

School Dinner
Saturday, 8:00 P.M.
Hank's Restaurant

Concert
FRIDAY, 8:00
AT PARKER HALL

GOAL   Ask about birthdays

2:28

1 🔊)) **VOCABULARY** • *Ordinal numbers* Read and listen. Then listen again and repeat.

1st first	**2nd** second	**3rd** third	**4th** fourth	**5th** fifth
6th sixth	**7th** seventh	**8th** eighth	**9th** ninth	**10th** tenth
11th eleventh	**12th** twelfth	**13th** thirteenth	**14th** fourteenth	**15th** fifteenth
16th sixteenth	**17th** seventeenth	**18th** eighteenth	**19th** nineteenth	**20th** twentieth
21st twenty-first	**22nd** twenty-second	**30th** thirtieth	**40th** fortieth	**50th** fiftieth

2 **PAIR WORK** Say a number. Your partner says the ordinal number.

❝ three ❞

❝ third ❞

2:29

3 🔊)) **VOCABULARY** • *Months of the year* Read and listen. Then listen again and repeat.

January	February	March	April	May	June
S M T W T F S	S M T W T F S	S M T W T F S	S M T W T F S	S M T W T F S	S M T W T F S
1 2 3 4	1	1	1 2 3 4 5	1 2 3	1 2 3 4 5 6 7
5 6 7 8 9 10 11	2 3 4 5 6 7 8	2 3 4 5 6 7 8	6 7 8 9 10 11 12	4 5 6 7 8 9 10	8 9 10 11 12 13 14
12 13 14 15 16 17 18	9 10 11 12 13 14 15	9 10 11 12 13 14 15	13 14 15 16 17 18 19	11 12 13 14 15 16 17	15 16 17 18 19 20 21
19 20 21 22 23 24 25	16 17 18 19 20 21 22	16 17 18 19 20 21 22	20 21 22 23 24 25 26	18 19 20 21 22 23 24	22 23 24 25 26 27 28
26 27 28 29 30 31	23 24 25 26 27 28	23 24 25 26 27 28 29	27 28 29 30	25 26 27 28 29 30 31	29 30
		30 31			

July	August	September	October	November	December
S M T W T F S	S M T W T F S	S M T W T F S	S M T W T F S	S M T W T F S	S M T W T F S
1 2 3 4 5	1 2	1 2 3 4 5 6	1 2 3 4	1	1 2 3 4 5 6
6 7 8 9 10 11 12	3 4 5 6 7 8 9	7 8 9 10 11 12 13	5 6 7 8 9 10 11	2 3 4 5 6 7 8	7 8 9 10 11 12 13
13 14 15 16 17 18 19	10 11 12 13 14 15 16	14 15 16 17 18 19 20	12 13 14 15 16 17 18	9 10 11 12 13 14 15	14 15 16 17 18 19 20
20 21 22 23 24 25 26	17 18 19 20 21 22 23	21 22 23 24 25 26 27	19 20 21 22 23 24 25	16 17 18 19 20 21 22	21 22 23 24 25 26 27
27 28 29 30 31	24 25 26 27 28 29 30	28 29 30	26 27 28 29 30 31	23 24 25 26 27 28 29	28 29 30 31
	31			30	

2:30

4 🔊)) **LISTENING COMPREHENSION** Listen to the dates. Circle the dates on the calendar.

5 **PAIR WORK** Say a date from the calendar. Your partner writes the date.

❝ July thirty-first ❞   *July 31st*

6 GRAMMAR • *Prepositions in, on, and at for dates and times: summary*

When's the party?	**In** January.
When's the meeting?	**On** Tuesday.
When's the dance?	**On** January 15th.
When's the dinner?	**On** the 12th.
What time's the movie?	**At** noon.
What time's the dance?	**At** 8:30.

Be careful!
in the morning
in the afternoon
in the evening
BUT **at** night

7 GRAMMAR PRACTICE Complete the sentences. Use *in*, *on*, or *at*.

1 The concert is .... July 14th .... 3:00 .... the afternoon.

2 The dinner is .... December .... the 6th.

3 The party is .... midnight .... Saturday.

4 The movie is .... November 1st .... 8:30 P.M.

5 The game is .... Wednesday .... noon.

6 The meeting is at the State Bank .... 11:00 .... the morning .... July 18th.

NOW YOU CAN Ask about birthdays

2:31
1 **CONVERSATION MODEL** Read and listen.

A: When's your birthday?

B: On July 15th. When's yours?

A: My birthday's in November. On the 13th.

2:32
2 **RHYTHM AND INTONATION** Listen again and repeat. Then practice the Conversation Model with a partner.

3 **PAIR WORK** Personalize the conversation with your own birthdays.

A: When's your birthday?

B: .... When's yours?

A: My birthday's ....

Don't stop!
Ask questions to complete the chart.

brother's birthday:	
sister's birthday:	
mother's birthday:	
father's birthday:	
grandmother's birthday:	
grandfather's birthday:	

4 **CHANGE PARTNERS** Ask about other people's birthdays.

2:33
 On someone's birthday say:

❝Happy birthday!❞   ❝Thank you!❞

Extension

More Practice
ActiveBook Self-Study Disc
grammar · vocabulary · listening
reading · speaking · pronunciation

1 2:34 **READING** Read the conversations. What are the events?

1 **A:** Hey, it's Alec's birthday on June 1st.
B: Really? That's on Friday.
A: That's right. And there's a party.
B: Great! Where?
A: At the New School, right around the corner.
B: What time?
A: 11:30.

2 **A:** There's a dance tomorrow at 10:30.
B: Hey, let's go! Where is it?
A: At Casey's Restaurant.
B: Is that next to the bookstore?
A: That's right.

3 **A:** There's a movie tonight at 8:00.
B: Really? What movie?
A: The Party, with Peter Sellers.
B: The English actor?
A: Right.
B: That's an old movie!
A: Yes, but it's good. Let's go. OK?

4 **A:** Where is the meeting?
B: At United Bank.
A: Can we walk there?
B: No, let's go by taxi.
A: Are we late?
B: No. The meeting's at 10:00. It's only 9:30.

2 **INTEGRATED PRACTICE** Correct all the mistakes. Use the information in the Reading.

1 The dance is at half past ~~nine~~ *ten*.
2 The movie is at 8:00 A.M.
3 The meeting is at half past ten.
4 The birthday party is at midnight.
5 Alec's birthday is in July.

6 The dance is at the bookstore.
7 The meeting is at the New School.
8 Alec's party is at United Bank.
9 United Bank is around the corner.
10 Peter Sellers is an English singer.

3 **GROUP WORK** Ask about classmates' birthdays. Complete the chart.

On your *ActiveBook* Self-Study Disc:
Extra Reading Comprehension Questions

GRAMMAR BOOSTER
Extra practice • p. 139

Capricorn
Dec. 22 – Jan. 20

Aquarius
Jan. 21–Feb. 19

Pisces
Feb. 20 – Mar. 20

Aries
Mar. 21 – Apr. 20

Taurus
Apr. 21– May 21

Sagittarius
Nov. 22 – Dec. 21

Name	Birthday	Zodiac Sign

Gemini
May 22 – Jun. 21

Scorpio
Oct. 23 – Nov. 21

Libra
Sep. 23 – Oct. 22

Virgo
Aug. 24 – Sep. 22

Leo
Jul. 23 – Aug. 23

Cancer
Jun. 22 – Jul. 22

2:35/2:36
Top Notch Pop
"Let's Make a Date"   Lyrics p. 147

PAIR WORK Create conversations for the people.

1 Talk about the events. For example:

Look. There's a ___ ...

2 Confirm that you are on time for an event. For example:

What time's the ___?

CONTEST Study the events for one minute. Then close your books. Who can remember all the times, dates, and locations? For example:

There's a ___ on ___ at ___.

WRITING Write five sentences about events at your school or in your city. For example:

There's a concert on Friday at ...

DINNER

When:
Friday, May 20th (8:30 P.M.)

Where:
My French Restaurant

Between the 13th Street School and the Corner Pharmacy

BASKETBALL GAME

**Sunday, May 22, noon
At the Twelfth Night School**

"Midnight" in Concert!

When:
10:30 P.M., Tuesday, May 24
Where: Paul's Books (Next to UMS Bank)

Party

Welcome all students!
**Saturday, May 28
9:30 P.M.**
Where? 58 Post Street
(across from the bank)

MAY 20 FRIDAY

NOW I CAN... ✓

- ☐ Confirm that I'm on time.
- ☐ Talk about the time of an event.
- ☐ Ask about birthdays.

43

GOALS After Unit 6, you will be able to:

1 Give and accept a compliment.
2 Ask for colors and sizes.
3 Describe clothes.

LESSON 1

GOAL Give and accept a compliment

VOCABULARY BOOSTER
More clothes • p. 129

1 🔊 **VOCABULARY** • *Clothes* Read and listen. Then listen again and repeat.

1 a shirt
2 a sweater
3 a tie
4 a jacket
5 a skirt
6 shoes
7 a dress
8 a suit
9 a blouse
10 pants*

* <u>Pants</u> is a plural noun. Use <u>are</u>, not <u>is</u>, with <u>pants</u>.

2 🔊 **PRONUNCIATION** • *Plurals* Read and listen. Then listen again and repeat.

1 /s/ **shirts** = shirt/s/   **2** /z/ **shoes** = shoe/z/   **3** /ɪz/ **blouses** = blouse/ɪz/
     jackets = jacket/s/   **sweaters** = sweater/z/   **dresses** = dress/ɪz/

3 GRAMMAR • *Demonstratives* <u>this</u>, <u>that</u>, <u>these</u>, <u>those</u>

this sweater   **that** sweater   **these** ties   **those** ties

4 GRAMMAR PRACTICE Look at the pictures. Write <u>this</u>, <u>that</u>, <u>these</u>, or <u>those</u> and the name of the clothes.

1 *those jackets*   2 ....   3 ....   4 ....

5 .... 6 .... 7 .... 8 ....

5 GRAMMAR • *The simple present tense: affirmative statements with* <u>like</u>, <u>want</u>, <u>need</u>, *and* <u>have</u>

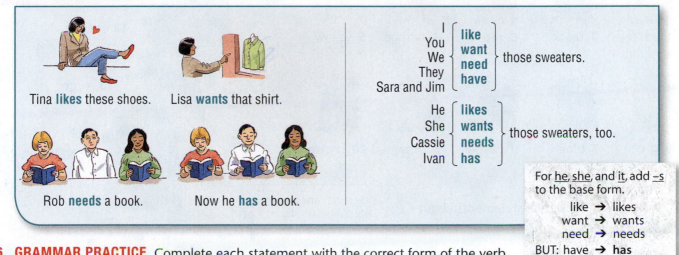

Tina **likes** these shoes. Lisa **wants** that shirt.

Rob **needs** a book. Now he **has** a book.

I You We They Sara and Jim	like want need have	} those sweaters.
He She Cassie Ivan	likes wants needs has	} those sweaters, too.

For <u>he</u>, <u>she</u>, and <u>it</u>, add –s to the base form.

like ➜ likes
want ➜ wants
need ➜ needs
BUT: have ➜ **has**

6 GRAMMAR PRACTICE Complete each statement with the correct form of the verb.

1 I .... your tie.
   like / likes

2 My friends .... this suit.
   want / wants

3 Janet .... this skirt.
   need / needs

4 Peter .... that jacket.
   have / has

5 We .... our dresses.
   like / likes

6 Sue and Tara .... those suits.
   want / wants

NOW YOU CAN Give and accept a compliment

1 🔊 **CONVERSATION MODEL** Read and listen. 2:39

A: I like that dress.
B: Thank you.
A: You're welcome.

2 🔊 **RHYTHM AND INTONATION** Listen again and repeat. 2:40
Then practice the Conversation Model with a partner.

3 PAIR WORK Personalize the conversation. Compliment
your classmates on their clothes and shoes. Then change roles.

A: I like ....
B: ....
A: You're welcome.

4 CHANGE PARTNERS Compliment other classmates' clothes.

45

GOAL   Ask for colors and sizes

1 🔊 **VOCABULARY** • *Colors and sizes* Read and listen. Then listen again and repeat.

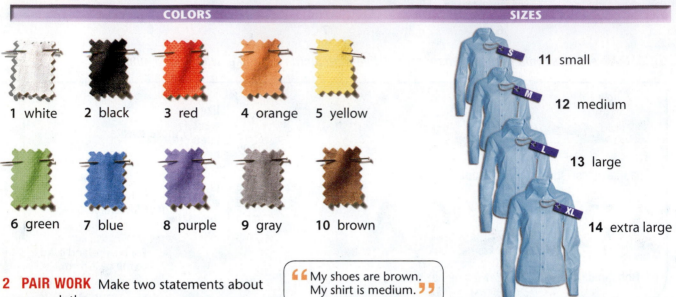

| COLORS | SIZES |

1 white   2 black   3 red   4 orange   5 yellow

6 green   7 blue   8 purple   9 gray   10 brown

11 small
12 medium
13 large
14 extra large

2 PAIR WORK Make two statements about your clothes.

> " My shoes are brown.
> My shirt is medium. "

3 GRAMMAR • *The simple present tense: negative statements and*
yes / no questions with like, want, need, and have

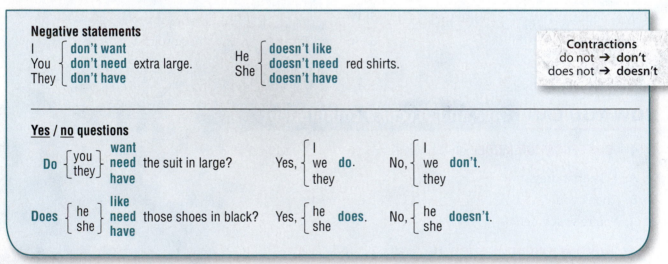

Negative statements

I
You   don't want
They   don't need   extra large.
       don't have

He   doesn't like
She   doesn't need   red shirts.
       doesn't have

Contractions
do not → **don't**
does not → **doesn't**

Yes / no questions

Do {you / they} **want / need / have** the suit in large?   Yes, {I / we / they} **do**.   No, {I / we / they} **don't**.

Does {he / she} **like / need / have** those shoes in black?   Yes, {he / she} **does**.   No, {he / she} **doesn't**.

4 GRAMMAR PRACTICE Complete the sentences with the correct form of the verb. Use contractions.

1 A: ....*Do*.... your children ...*have*... sweaters for
have
   school?

   B: My daughter ...*does*..., but my son ...*doesn't*... .

2 A: .... your husband .... a black tie?
need

   B: No, he .... He .... two black ties.
have

3 A: I .... a blue suit for work. .... you
need
   .... one too?
need

   B: Yes, I ....

4 A: .... you .... that green
like
   shirt?

   B: Actually, no, I ....

5 A: We .... the clothes in this store.
not like

   B: Really, that's too bad. We ....

6 A: .... you .... this black jacket in
have
   size 34?

   B: No, I'm sorry. We ....

5  **LISTENING COMPREHENSION** Listen to the conversations about clothes. For each statement, circle T (true) or F (false). Then listen again and circle the color.

T F **1** They like the dress.

T F **2** He needs shoes.

T F **3** Matt needs a suit for work.

T F **4** He needs a tie.

T F **5** She needs the sweater in small.

T F **6** They don't have his size.

NOW YOU CAN   Ask for colors and sizes

1  **CONVERSATION MODEL** Read and listen.

A: Do you have this sweater in green?

B: Yes, we do.

A: Great. And my husband needs a shirt. Do you have that shirt in large?

B: No, I'm sorry. We don't.

A: That's too bad.

2  **RHYTHM AND INTONATION** Listen again and repeat. Then practice the Conversation Model with a partner.

3 PAIR WORK Now change the model. Ask for colors and sizes of clothes for you and a member of your family. Use the pictures. Then change roles.

A: Do you have .... in ....?

B: ....

A: .... And my .... needs .... Do you have .... in ....?

B: ....

A: ....

4 CHANGE PARTNERS Practice the conversation again. Ask about other clothes.

47

GOAL   Describe clothes

2:45
1 🔊 **VOCABULARY** • *Opposite adjectives to describe clothes* Read and listen. Then listen again and repeat.

| 1 new | 2 old | 3 dirty | 4 clean |

| 5 loose | 6 tight | 7 cheap | 8 expensive |

9 long   10 short

2 GRAMMAR • *Adjective placement*

> **Adjectives come before the nouns they describe.**
> a **long** skirt   **tight** shoes   a **red** and **black** tie
>
> **Adjectives don't change.**
> a **clean** shirt / **clean** shirts NOT ~~cleans~~ shirts.
>
> **Be careful!**
> It's a **long skirt**. NOT It's a ~~skirt long~~.

3 PAIR WORK Look at your classmates. Take turns describing their clothes.

❝ Allen has new shoes. ❞

❝ Joe's shoes are old.
He needs new shoes. ❞

4 GRAMMAR PRACTICE Write two descriptions for each picture. Follow the model.

1 The _blouses_ are _clean_ .
   They're _clean blouses_ .

2 The .... is ....
   It's ....

3 The .... are ....
   They're ....

5 GRAMMAR • *The simple present tense: questions with <u>What</u>, <u>Why</u>, and <u>Which</u> / <u>One</u> and <u>ones</u>*

Use a question word and <u>do</u> or <u>does</u> to ask information questions in the simple present tense.
What **do** you **need**? (A blue and white tie.)   What **does** she **want**? (New shoes.)

Use <u>because</u> to answer questions with <u>Why</u>.
Why **do** they **want** that suit? (**Because** it's nice.)   Why **does** he **like** this tie? (**Because** it's green.)

Use <u>Which</u> to ask about choice. Answer with <u>one</u> or <u>ones</u>.
Which sweater **do** you **want**? (The blue **one**.)   Which shoes **does** she **like**? (The black **ones**.)

6 GRAMMAR PRACTICE Complete the conversations. Answer each question in your own words.
Then practice the conversations with a partner.

1 A: Which skirt ....?
     she / want
   B: The .... one.

2 A: What ....?
     your friend / need
   B: ....

3 A: What color shoes ....?
     you / like
   B: ....

4 A: Why .... new shoes?
     you / want
   B: ....

5 A: Which shirts ....?
     you / like
   B: The .... ones.

6 A: What size shoes ....?
     you / need
   B: ....

NOW YOU CAN Describe clothes

1 🔊 2:46 **CONVERSATION MODEL** Read and listen.

A: What do you think of this jacket?
B: I think it's nice. What about you?
A: Well, it's nice, but it's a little tight.
B: Let's keep looking.

2 🔊 2:47 **RHYTHM AND INTONATION** Listen again and repeat.
Then practice the Conversation Model with a partner.

3 **PAIR WORK** Now change the model. Use different
clothes. Use different problems. Then change roles.

A: What do you think of ....?
B: I think .... nice. What about you?
A: Well, ... nice, but .... a little ....
B: Let's keep looking.

♻ **Be sure to recycle this language.**

Clothes		Problems
shirt	pants	expensive
sweater	skirt	tight
dress	jacket	loose
tie	shoes	long
		short

4 **CHANGE PARTNERS** Talk about different clothes and problems.

More Practice
ActiveBook *Self-Study Disc*
grammar · vocabulary · listening
reading · speaking · pronunciation

1 🔊 2:48 **READING** Read the advertisement from today's newspaper. Which clothes do you like?

TODAY ONLY!
1/2 Price Sale

THE EMPORIUM
A Great Clothes Store!

Low, Low Prices!
MEN'S & WOMEN'S CLOTHES
ALL STORES OPEN UNTIL MIDNIGHT

Many more styles available.

Blue at King Street store only.

White not available at South Street Station location.

Other sale items today: Children's jackets and shoes
STORE LOCATIONS: 62 KING STREET, THE UPTOWN MALL, AND SOUTH STREET STATION.

2 READING COMPREHENSION Read the statements about the advertisement. Check <u>True</u> or <u>False</u>.

	True	False
1 The sale is every day this week.	☐	☐
2 The store has three locations.	☐	☐
3 The Emporium is a clothes store.	☐	☐
4 White blouses are on sale at two locations.	☐	☐

	True	False
5 All locations have blue sweaters.	☐	☐
6 The Emporium doesn't have children's shoes.	☐	☐

On your *ActiveBook* Self-Study Disc:
Extra Reading Comprehension Questions

3 PAIR WORK Discuss the sale at the Emporium. Use the advertisement.

♻ **Be sure to recycle this language.**

Do you want ___ ?
Do you like this / that ___ ?
Do you need [a gray] ___ ?
What do you need / like / want / have?
Which ___ do you ___ ?
Why do you ___ these / those ___ ?

❝ What do you need? ❞

❝ I need a white blouse for work, and my children need shoes for school. Let's go to the Emporium. They have a great sale. ❞

GRAMMAR BOOSTER
Extra practice • p. 140

GAME Describe people's clothes. Your partner points to the picture. For example:

He has a yellow shirt.

PAIR WORK

1 Point and ask and answer questions about the picture. Use <u>this</u> / <u>that</u> / <u>these</u> / <u>those</u> and <u>like</u>, <u>want</u>, <u>need</u>, and <u>have</u>. For example:

Do you like these shoes?

2 Create conversations for the people. For example:

A: Do you want these pants?
B: No, I don't.

WRITING Write about clothes you need, you want, you like, and clothes you have or don't have. For example:

I need a new white blouse. My old blouse is a little tight. I want red shoes and a long skirt...

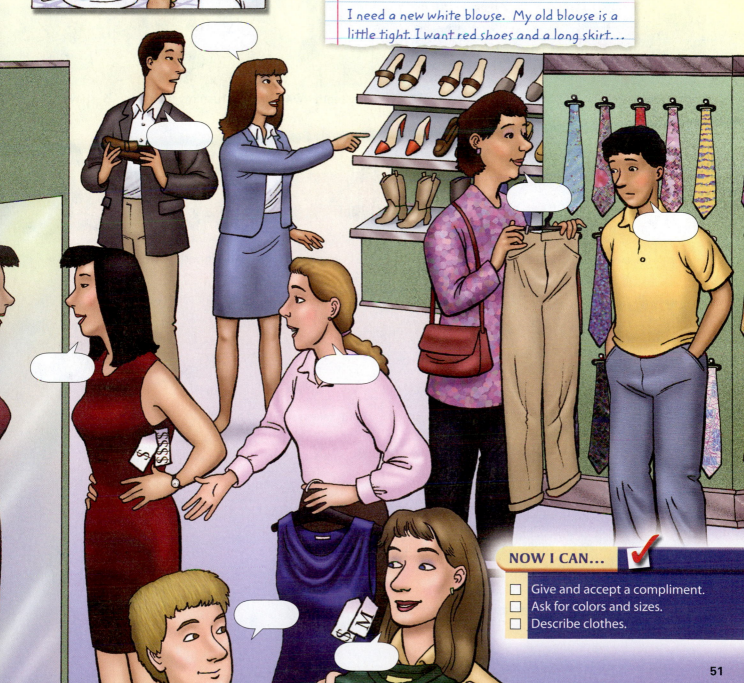

NOW I CAN... ✔

- ☐ Give and accept a compliment.
- ☐ Ask for colors and sizes.
- ☐ Describe clothes.

GOALS After Unit 7, you will be able to:

1 Talk about morning and evening activities.
2 Describe what you do in your free time.
3 Discuss household chores.

LESSON 1

| GOAL | Talk about morning and evening activities |

3:02
1 VOCABULARY • *Daily activities at home* Read and listen. Then listen again and repeat.

1 get up

2 get dressed

3 brush my teeth

4 comb / brush my hair

5 shave

6 put on makeup

7 eat breakfast

8 come home

9 make dinner

10 study

11 watch TV

12 get undressed

13 take a shower / a bath

14 go to bed

2 PAIR WORK Tell your partner about your daily activities.

" I eat lunch at 12:00. "

3:03
Meals
breakfast
lunch
dinner

3 GRAMMAR • *The simple present tense: spelling rules with <u>he</u>, <u>she</u>, and <u>it</u>*

Add –s to the base form of most verbs
gets   shaves   combs

Add –es to verbs that end in –s, –sh, –ch, or –x.
brushes   watches

Remember:
do → does
go → goes
have → has
study → studies

4 GRAMMAR PRACTICE Complete the statements. Use the simple present tense.

1 Tom .... up at 6:00, but his wife, Kate,
   get
.... up at 7:00.
   get

2 Kate .... breakfast at 7:30 A.M., but
   eat
Tom .... breakfast at 6:30.
   eat

3 After breakfast, Tom ...., and Kate
   shave
.... on makeup.
   put

4 Tom and Kate .... TV in the evening.
   watch

5 Kate .... to bed at 10:00 P.M., but
   go
Tom .... to bed at 11:00.
   go

6 Kate .... dinner on weekdays, and
   make
Tom .... dinner on weekends.
   make

7 Tom .... a shower in the morning, but
   take
Kate .... a bath.
   take

8 Tom and Kate .... their teeth in the morning
   brush
and in the evening.

5 GRAMMAR • *The simple present tense: questions with <u>When</u> and <u>What time</u>*

When **do** you **take** a shower? (In the morning.)
What time **does** she **get** up? (Before 7:00 A.M.)

before 8:00 **7:45** | after 8:00 **8:15**

6 GRAMMAR PRACTICE On a separate sheet of paper, write five questions about Tom and Kate in Exercise 4. Then listen to and answer a classmate's questions aloud.

1 What time does Kate get up?

" She gets up at 7:00. "

| NOW YOU CAN | **Talk about morning and evening activities** |

3:04
1 🔊 **CONVERSATION MODEL** Read and listen.

A: Are you a morning person or an evening person?

B: Me? I'm definitely an evening person.

A: And why do you say that?

B: Well, I get up after ten in the morning. And I go to bed after two. What about you?

A: I'm a morning person. I get up before six.

3:05
2 🔊 **RHYTHM AND INTONATION** Listen again and repeat. Then practice the Conversation Model with a partner.

3 PAIR WORK Personalize the conversation. Use your own information.

A: Are you a morning person or an evening person?

B: Me? I'm definitely ....

A: And why do you say that?

B: Well, I .... What about you?

A: I'm .... I ....

4 CHANGE PARTNERS Personalize the conversation again.

5 CLASS SURVEY Find out how many students are morning people and how many are evening people.

Don't stop!
Ask more questions.

♻ **Be sure to recycle this language.**

When do you ___ ?
What time do you ___ ?
What about your [parents]?

GOAL **Describe what you do in your free time**

1 🔊 **VOCABULARY** • *Leisure activities* Read and listen. Then listen again and repeat.

1 exercise

2 take a nap

3 listen to music

4 read

5 play soccer

6 check e-mail

7 go out for dinner

8 go to the movies

9 go dancing

10 visit friends

2 **INTEGRATED PRACTICE** Write six questions for a classmate about his or her leisure activities. Use <u>When</u> or <u>What time</u> and the simple present tense.

> 1 *When do you visit friends?*

1		4	
2		5	
3		6	

3 **GRAMMAR** • *The simple present tense: frequency adverbs*

100% ⬆ I **always** play soccer on Saturday.
I **usually** check e-mail in the evening.
I **sometimes** go dancing on weekends.
0% ⬇ I **never** take a nap in the afternoon.

Be careful!
Place the frequency adverb before the verb in the simple present tense.

Don't say: I ~~play always~~ soccer.
He ~~checks usually~~ e-mail.

4 **PAIR WORK** Now use your questions from Exercise 2 to ask your partner about leisure activities. Use frequency adverbs and time expressions in your answers.

❝ When do you visit friends? ❞

❝ I usually visit friends on Saturday. ❞

5 GRAMMAR PRACTICE Write sentences about your partner from Exercise 4 on a separate sheet of paper.

Scott usually visits friends on Saturday.

1 🔊 3:07 **CONVERSATION MODEL** Read and listen.

A: What's your typical day like?

B: Well, I usually go to work at 9:00 and come home at 6:00.

A: And what do you do in your free time?

B: I sometimes read or watch TV. What about you?

A: Pretty much the same.

2 🔊 3:08 **RHYTHM AND INTONATION** Listen again and repeat. Then practice the Conversation Model with a partner.

3 PAIR WORK Write your typical daily activities on the notepad. Then personalize the conversation with your own information.

A: What's your typical day like?

B: Well, I ....

A: And what do you do in your free time?

B: .... What about you?

A: ....

> **Don't stop!**
> Ask about other times and days.

♻️ **Be sure to recycle this language.**

Time expressions

in the morning	at night
in the afternoon	on [Friday]
in the evening	

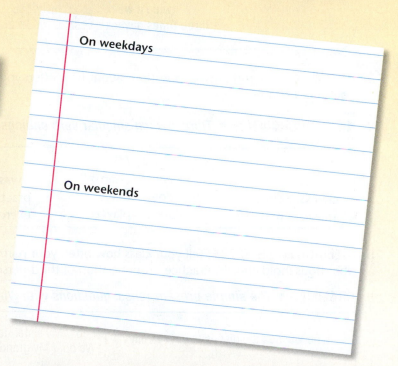

On weekdays

On weekends

4 CHANGE PARTNERS Personalize the conversation again.

5 GROUP WORK Tell the class about your partner's activities.

55

GOAL Discuss household chores

VOCABULARY BOOSTER
More household chores • p. 129

1 🔊 3:09 **VOCABULARY** • *Household chores* Read and listen. Then listen again and repeat.

1 wash the dishes

2 clean the house

3 do the laundry

4 take out the garbage

5 go shopping

2 **GRAMMAR** • *The simple present tense: questions with <u>How often</u> / Other time expressions*

How often **do** you **take** out the garbage?	M	T	W	T	F	S	S
I take out the garbage **every day**.	✓	✓	✓	✓	✓	✓	✓

	M	T	W	T	F	S	S
How often **does** she **go** shopping?						✓	
She goes shopping **on Saturdays**.						✓	

Other time expressions	M	T	W	T	F	S	S
once a week	✓						
twice a week		✓		✓			
three times a week		✓		✓	✓		

Also
- once a year
- twice a day
- three times a month
- every weekend
- every Friday

3 **PAIR WORK** Ask and answer questions about how often you do household chores.

❝ How often do you go shopping? ❞

❝ Twice a week. ❞

4 🔊 3:10 **PRONUNCIATION** • *Third-person singular verb endings* Read and listen. Then listen again and repeat.

1 /s/	**2** /z/	**3** /ɪz/
take**s** = take/s/	clean**s** = clean/z/	wash**es** = wash/ɪz/
check**s** = check/s/	doe**s** = doe/z/	practic**es** = practice/ɪz/
make**s** = make/s/	play**s** = play/z/	exercis**es** = exercise/ɪz/

5 **INTEGRATED PRACTICE** Tell your class how often your partner from Exercise 3 does household chores. Practice pronunciation of third-person verb endings.

❝ John **goes** shopping twice a week. ❞

6 **GRAMMAR** • *The simple present tense: questions with <u>Who</u> as subject*

Who washes the dishes in your family? ⎰ I do. / My sister does.
⎱ We do. / My grandparents do.

Be careful!
Always use a third-person singular verb when <u>who</u> is the subject.
   Don't say: Who ~~clean~~ the house?
Don't use <u>do</u> or <u>does</u> when <u>who</u> is the subject.
   Don't say: Who ~~does clean~~ the house?

7 ◀») **LISTENING COMPREHENSION** Listen to the conversations and the questions with <u>Who</u>. Check the chores each person does.

1	She…	○	○	○	○	○
	Her husband…	○	○	○	○	○
	Her son…	○	○	○	○	○
	Her daughter…	○	○	○	○	○
2	He…	○	○	○	○	○
	His brother…	○	○	○	○	○
	His sister…	○	○	○	○	○
3	She…	○	○	○	○	○
	Her husband…	○	○	○	○	○
4	He…	○	○	○	○	○
	His wife…	○	○	○	○	○
	His son…	○	○	○	○	○

8 **GRAMMAR PRACTICE** With a partner, ask and answer questions about the people in Exercise 7.

❝ In Conversation 1, who washes the dishes? ❞

❝ Her husband does. ❞

NOW YOU CAN **Discuss household chores**

1 ◀») **CONVERSATION MODEL** Read and listen.
3:12

A: So how often do you do the laundry?

B: About twice a week. How about you?

A: Me? I never do the laundry. Could I ask another question?

B: Sure.

A: Who cleans the house?

B: Oh, that's my brother's job.

2 ◀») **RHYTHM AND INTONATION** Listen again and repeat.
3:13
Then practice the Conversation Model with a partner.
Then change roles.

3 **PAIR WORK** Personalize the conversation.

A: So how often do you ....?

B: .... How about you?

A: Me? .... Could I ask another question?

B: ....

A: Who ....?

B: Oh, that's .... 's job.

Don't stop!
Ask about other chores.

4 **CHANGE PARTNERS** Ask another classmate about household chores.

5 **GROUP WORK** Tell your classmates about your partner's household chores.

1 3:14 🔊 **READING** Read the article. Do you like housework?

Don't like household chores?
These robots help!

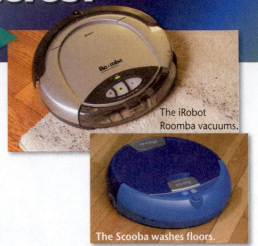

The iRobot
Roomba vacuums.

The Scooba washes floors.

How often do you clean your house? Once a week? Twice a month? Never? Well, these two robots clean the house for you. The iRobot Roomba turns right or left, and vacuums while you watch TV or exercise. Take a nap, and the house is clean when you get up. And if you want to wash the floor, the iRobot Scooba washes the floor for you. The Scooba moves around corners and washes the floor while you listen to music or check your e-mail. Now that's help with household chores!

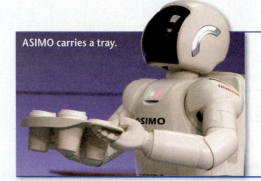

ASIMO carries a tray.

And who is this? Meet ASIMO, a robot from the Honda Motor Company. ASIMO doesn't clean the house. It doesn't wash dishes or take out the garbage. But ASIMO walks and carries things. Say "turn left" or "turn right," and ASIMO turns.

No one wants to mow the lawn. But the L200 Evolution lawn mower mows the lawn for you. Tell the robot what time you want to mow. How about midnight, after you go to bed? It mows the lawn while you sleep. How about in the afternoon? It mows the lawn while you go out for lunch or go shopping.

The L200 mows lawns.

Sources: www.irobot.com, world.honda.com/ASIMO, www.robotlawnmowers.ie

2 READING COMPREHENSION Complete each statement. Circle the correct verb.

1 The Roomba (washes / vacuums /mows).

2 The Scooba (washes / vacuums / mows).

3 The Roomba and the Scooba (wash / clean / vacuum).

4 The L200 Evolution (washes / mows / cleans).

5 ASIMO (washes / mows / walks).

3 INTEGRATED PRACTICE On a separate sheet of paper, write five sentences about the robots. Use the simple present tense.

4 DISCUSSION Which robots do you like? Do you want any of them? Why?

> " I want the Roomba because it cleans the house. "

On your *ActiveBook* Self-Study Disc:
Extra Reading Comprehension Questions

GRAMMAR BOOSTER
Extra practice • p. 140

3:15–3:16
🎵 **Top Notch Pop**
"On the Weekend" Lyrics p. 147

Jack's Typical Day

Morning

7:00 A.M.

7:10 A.M.

7:45 A.M.

8:15 A.M.

8:30 A.M.

Evening

6:00 P.M.

6:30 P.M.

7:00 P.M.

7:30 P.M.

8:00 P.M.

10:15

11:00 P.M.

CONTEST Study the photos for one minute. Then close your books. Who remembers all Jack's activities?

PAIR WORK Create a conversation for Jack and a friend. Start like this:

    Jack, are you a morning person or an evening person? OR: What's your typical day like?

TRUE OR FALSE? Make statements about Jack's activities. Your partner says <u>True</u> or <u>False</u>. Take turns. For example:

    A: Jack usually takes a shower in the evening.
    B: False. He takes a shower in the morning.

WRITING Describe <u>your</u> typical week. Use adverbs of frequency and time expressions. For example:

    I exercise every weekend.

NOW I CAN... ✔

- ☐ Talk about morning and evening activities.
- ☐ Describe what I do in my free time.
- ☐ Discuss household chores.

1 🔊))) **LISTENING COMPREHENSION** Listen to the conversations. Check each statement T (true) or F (false). Then listen again and check your work.

T F

☐ ☐ **1** She's a manager.

☐ ☐ **2** He's a doctor.

☐ ☐ **3** She's an architect.

T F

☐ ☐ **4** He's a student.

☐ ☐ **5** They're artists.

☐ ☐ **6** She's his neighbor.

2 **PAIR WORK** Ask and answer questions about places on the maps.

   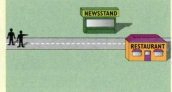

3 **GRAMMAR PRACTICE** Complete each sentence with <u>in</u>, <u>on</u>, or <u>at</u>.

1 The movie is .... Friday .... 8:00.

2 The meeting is .... June 6th .... the morning.

3 The party is .... Saturday .... midnight.

4 The dinner is .... April.

5 The dance is .... 8:00 P.M. .... Friday.

4 **GRAMMAR PRACTICE** Complete the sentences with <u>this</u>, <u>that</u>, <u>these</u>, or <u>those</u>.

1 I want .... pants.

2 I like .... jackets.

3 I like .... suit.

4 I want .... tie.

5 **PAIR WORK**

Partner A: Ask these questions. Partner B: Read the correct response to each question aloud.

1 Does he have grandchildren?
  a Yes, he has two sons.
  b Yes, he does.

2 Where's the pharmacy?
  a Don't walk. Take the bus.
  b It's around the corner.

3 Are we late?
  a Yes, you're early.
  b Yes. It's 10:00.

Partner B: Ask these questions. Partner A: Read the correct response to each question aloud.

4 When's the dance?
  a On Saturday.
  b At the school.

5 Do you like this suit?
  a Yes, I do.
  b Yes, it is.

6 How do you go to work?
  a I walk.
  b Walk.

6 PAIR WORK Write your own response to each person. Then practice your conversations with a partner.

1 *Hi. I'm John.* YOU *Nice to meet you* .

2 *What's your last name?* YOU ....

3 *Do you have children?* YOU ....

4 *What time is it?* YOU ....

5 *When's your birthday?* YOU ....

6 *What do you do?* YOU ....

7 GRAMMAR PRACTICE Look at the pictures. Write an imperative for each.

1 ....*Walk*......... to the bank. **2** .... to work. **3** .... to the pharmacy.

4 .... to the restaurant. **5** .... to school. **6** .... to the bookstore.

8 CONVERSATION PRACTICE With a partner, exchange real information about your families. Start like this:

❝ Tell me about your family. ❞

Ideas
Ask about names.   Ask about occupations.
Ask about ages.   Describe people.

9 🔊 **LISTENING COMPREHENSION** Listen to the conversations. Answer the questions.
Then listen again and check your work.

1	What's her phone number?	It's __ __ __ __ __ __ __ __ __ __ .
2	What's his last name?	It's __ __ __ __ __ __ .
3	How old is his son?	He's __ years old.
4	What's the address?	It's __ __ West 12th Street.
5	What time is it?	It's 2: __ __ .

10 GRAMMAR PRACTICE Circle the correct word or words to complete each statement or question.

1 Is he (your / you) husband?

2 Is she (their / they) granddaughter?

3 (Her / His) name is Mr. Grant.

4 (Our / We) birthdays are in May.

5 How do you spell (her / she) name?

6 I'm (Ms. Bell / Ms. Bell's) student.

11 INTEGRATED PRACTICE Write a question for each response.

1 A: ....?
B: No. She's a student.

2 A: ....?
B: I'm an architect.

3 A: ....?
B: The bank is across the street.

4 A: ....?
B: It's 9:45.

5 A: ....?
B: It's 34 Bank Street.

6 A: ....?
B: The newsstand is around the corner.

7 A: ....?
B: My birthday? In February.

8 A: ....?
B: They're my sisters.

12 PAIR WORK

Partner A: Ask these questions. Partner B: Read the correct response to each question aloud.

1 Does Jack have a large family?
a Yes, I do.
b Yes, he does.

2 Does her father shave every morning?
a Yes, he is.
b No, he doesn't.

3 Is Ms. Wang his English teacher?
a Yes, he is.
b Yes, she is.

Partner B: Ask these questions. Partner A: Read the correct response to each question aloud.

4 Does she like red shoes?
a No, she doesn't.
b Yes, I do.

5 Does he need a new tie?
a Yes, he does.
b Yes, I do.

6 Does she always clean the house on Sunday?
a Yes, she is.
b Yes, she does.

13 GRAMMAR PRACTICE Circle the correct verb to complete each sentence.

1 We (am / are) friends.

2 They (has / have) two children.

3 Who (has / have) a blue suit?

4 (Do / Does) she (want / wants) new shoes?

5 Why (do / does) they (need / needs) new shoes?

6 (Is / Are) we on time?

14 GRAMMAR PRACTICE Complete the statements with verbs in the simple present tense.

1 I usually .... TV in the evening, but my brother .... to music.

2 We sometimes .... the house and .... the laundry in the morning.

3 After dinner, I always .... the dishes and my wife .... out the garbage.

4 My neighbors never .... shopping on weekdays.

5 My sister always .... to bed before 10:00 P.M., but I usually .... e-mail at 10:00.

6 My grandfather always .... a nap in the afternoon.

15 INTEGRATED PRACTICE On a separate sheet of paper, answer the questions. Use frequency adverbs or time expressions. Then tell your classmates about your activities.

1 What do you do on weekends?

2 What do you do after breakfast?

3 What do you do after work or school?

4 What do you do at night before you go to bed?

1   I usually go shopping on weekends.

16 CONVERSATION PRACTICE With a partner, talk about the times of events. Use the pictures or your own ideas. Start like this:

❝ Look. There's a ___ on ___. ❞

 Be sure to recycle this language.

Really?
What time?
Let's go!
Good idea.
across the street
down the street
around the corner

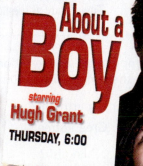

BASKETBALL GAME
BRAZIL and CANADA
Saturday, 8:30 P.M.

WEEKEND CONCERT
THE TOKYO STRINGS
SUNDAY, 3:30 P.M.

ENGLISH MOVIE FESTIVAL
About a Boy
starring
Hugh Grant
THURSDAY, 6:00

Other events
a meeting
a party
a dance
a dinner
your own idea ___

Home and Neighborhood

GOALS After Unit 8, you will be able to:
1 Describe your neighborhood.
2 Ask about someone's home.
3 Talk about furniture and appliances.

LESSON 1

GOAL	Describe your neighborhood

3:19

1 🔊 **VOCABULARY** • *Buildings* Read and listen. Then listen again and repeat.

1 a house	2 an apartment building	3 an office building

6 a stairway
7 an apartment
8 a balcony

4 a garden   5 a garage

9 an elevator
11 the third floor
12 the second floor
13 the first floor
10 an office

2 **GRAMMAR** • *The simple present tense: questions with Where / Prepositions of place*

Questions with Where

Where **do** { you / your parents } **live**?   Where **does** { he / your mother } **work**?

Prepositions of place

in
She lives **in** an apartment.
They live **in** a house.
I work **in** an office.

at
I live **at** 50 Main Street.
He works **at** the bookstore.
They study **at** the new English School.

on
Her house is **on** Bank Street.
We go to school **on** 34th Avenue.
I work **on** the tenth floor.

3 **GRAMMAR PRACTICE** Complete the conversations. Use prepositions of place and the verb <u>be</u> or the simple present tense.

1 A: Where .... your sister's apartment?

   B: Her apartment .... Green Street.

2 A: Where .... you .... English?

   B: We study .... the school around the corner.

3 A: .... your neighbor .... a bank?

   B: No. She works .... a bookstore.

4 A: Where .... your parents ....?

   B: They live .... 58 Gray Street.

3:20

4 🔊 **PRONUNCIATION** • *Linking sounds* Read and listen. Then listen and repeat.

1 It's on First Avenue.

2 She works at home.

3 He lives in an apartment.

4 My friend studies at home.

5 INTEGRATED PRACTICE Ask and answer questions with <u>Where</u> about your partner's relatives. Practice linking sounds in your answers.

" Where does your father work? "

" He works at a bank. "

3:21
6 🔊 VOCABULARY • *Places in the neighborhood* Read and listen. Then listen again and repeat.

3:22
🔊 **Preposition <u>near</u>**

Train Station

Bus Station

The bus station is **near** the train station. It's right across the street.

1 a bus station

2 a train station

3 a stadium

4 a park

5 a mall

6 a museum

7 an airport

8 a hospital

NOW YOU CAN | **Describe your neighborhood**

3:23
1 🔊 CONVERSATION MODEL Read and listen.

A: Do you live far from here?

B: No. About fifteen minutes by bus.

A: And is the neighborhood nice?

B: Yes, it is. My apartment is near a park and a mall.

A: Really? My apartment is next to an airport!

3:24
2 🔊 RHYTHM AND INTONATION Listen again and repeat. Then practice the Conversation Model with a partner.

3 PAIR WORK Personalize the conversation.

A: Do you .... far from here?

B: ....

A: And is the neighborhood nice?

B: ...., it .... My .... is ....

A: Really? My .... is ....

Don't stop!
Describe more places in your neighborhood. Ask questions with <u>Where</u>.

Where do you [go shopping]?
Where do you [go out for dinner]?

4 CHANGE PARTNERS Ask about another classmate's neighborhood.

GOAL   Ask about someone's home

3:25

1 🔊 **VOCABULARY** • *Rooms* Read and listen. Then listen again and repeat.

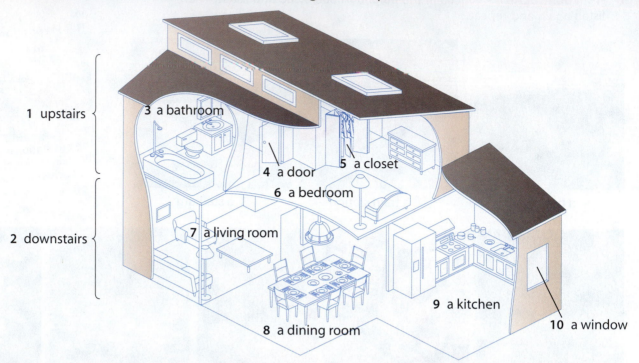

1 upstairs
   3 a bathroom
   4 a door
   5 a closet
   6 a bedroom

2 downstairs
   7 a living room
   8 a dining room
   9 a kitchen
   10 a window

2 PAIR WORK Tell your partner about the rooms in your home.

> "My apartment has one large bedroom and two small bedrooms."

3 GRAMMAR • *There is* and *there are* / Questions with *How many*

There is and There are
Use **there is** with singular nouns. Use **there are** with plural nouns.

There's a small bedroom downstairs.
There's a large closet and two windows.
There's no kitchen.

There are three large bedrooms upstairs.
There are two windows and a large closet.
There are no elevators.

Is there a balcony? { Yes, **there is.**
                No, **there isn't.**

Are there closets? { Yes, **there are.**
             No, **there aren't.**

> there is → **there's**
> BUT there are NOT ~~there're~~

> **Be careful!**
> Yes, there is.
> NOT Yes, ~~there's.~~

How many
Ask questions about quantity with **How many**. Always use a plural noun with **How many**.

How many bathrooms **are there**? (There are two.)
How many bedrooms **do** you **have**? (We have three.)

---

4 GRAMMAR PRACTICE Complete the sentences. Use <u>there's</u>, <u>there are</u>, <u>is there</u>, or <u>are there</u>.

1 How many closets ...*are there*... in the house?
2 .... a small bedroom downstairs.
3 .... a balcony on the second floor?
4 .... an elevator and two stairways.

5 .... a garden next to her house.
6 .... two bedrooms upstairs.
7 .... a park near my apartment.
8 How many windows .... ?

5 GRAMMAR PRACTICE On a separate sheet of paper, write ten sentences about your house or apartment. Use <u>There is</u> and <u>There are</u>.

> There's a small bathroom next to my bedroom.

3:26

6 ◀))) **LISTENING COMPREHENSION** Listen to the conversations. Check the best house or apartment for each person.

---

http://www.homeawayfromhome.com

Home Away from Home
Live in a house or apartment overseas for 1 to 6 months!
🏛 Call us at 1-800-555-9038 🏛

1. **Paris**
☐ A two-bedroom house with a large kitchen
☐ A one-bedroom apartment with a small kitchen

2. **Buenos Aires**
☐ A two-bedroom house with three bathrooms
☐ A two-bedroom house with two bathrooms

3. **Tokyo**
☐ A one-bedroom apartment with a large kitchen
☐ A one-bedroom apartment with a large closet

4. **Montreal**
☐ A two-bedroom house with a small garden
☐ A two-bedroom apartment with a balcony

NOW YOU CAN   Ask about someone's home

3:27

1 ◀))) **CONVERSATION MODEL** Read and listen.

A: Do you live in a house or an apartment?

B: An apartment.

A: What's it like?

B: Well, there are three large bedrooms, and it has a large kitchen.

A: Sounds nice!

3:28

2 ◀))) **RHYTHM AND INTONATION** Listen again and repeat. Then practice the Conversation Model with a partner.

3 **PAIR WORK** Personalize the conversation. Describe your house or apartment to your partner. Then change roles.

A: Do you live in a house or an apartment?

B: ....

A: What's it like?

B: Well, ...

A: Sounds nice!

Don't stop!
Ask more questions.
Is there ___ ?
Are there ___ ?
How many ___ ?

4 **CHANGE PARTNERS** Talk about another classmate's home.

GOAL   Talk about furniture and appliances

1 3:29 🔊 **VOCABULARY • *Furniture and appliances*** First write the name of each room (a-f). Then read and listen. Listen again and repeat.

a | *an office*

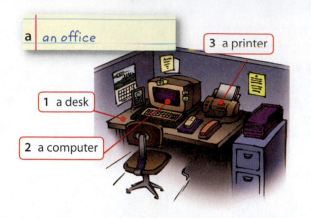

3 a printer
1 a desk
2 a computer

b

4 a dresser
6 a lamp
5 a bed
7 a rug

c

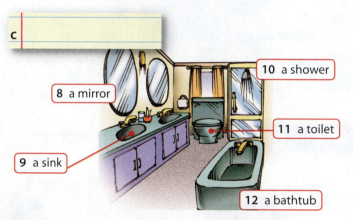

8 a mirror
10 a shower
9 a sink
11 a toilet
12 a bathtub

d

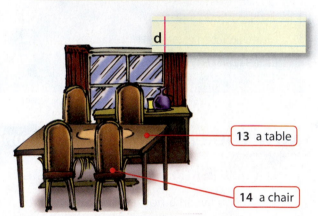

13 a table
14 a chair

e

16 a bookcase
15 a TV
17 a sofa

f

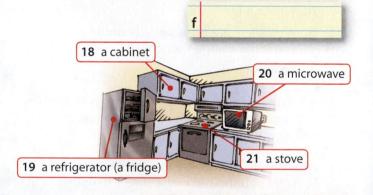

18 a cabinet
20 a microwave
19 a refrigerator (a fridge)
21 a stove

> **VOCABULARY BOOSTER**
> *More home and office vocabulary • p. 130*

2 3:30 🔊 **LISTENING COMPREHENSION** Listen to the comments about furniture and appliances. Look at the pictures in the Vocabulary. Write the correct room.

1 It's in the ....   **4** It's in the ....

2 It's in the ....   **5** It's in the ....

3 It's in the ....   **6** It's in the ....

3 PAIR WORK Ask your partner about the furniture and appliances in his or her home.

> " What's in your living room? "

> " My living room has a sofa and two chairs, and there's a large bookcase. "

NOW YOU CAN Talk about furniture and appliances

1 🔊 3:31 **CONVERSATION MODEL** Read and listen.

A: This is a nice sofa. What do you think?

B: Actually, I think it's beautiful.

A: And what about this lamp?

B: I don't know. I'm not sure.

2 🔊 3:32 **RHYTHM AND INTONATION**
Listen again and repeat. Then practice the Conversation Model with a partner.

🔊 3:33 **Positive and negative adjectives**

☺
beautiful
nice
great

☹
ugly
awful
terrible

3 PAIR WORK Change the model. Ask your partner's opinion about the furniture and appliances in the pictures. (Or use your own pictures.) Then change roles.

A: This is a nice .... What do you think?

B: Actually, I think it's ....

A: And what about this ....?

B: ....

Don't stop!
Ask about other furniture and appliances.

♻ **Be sure to recycle this language.**

I like this __ .
I don't like this __ .

4 CHANGE PARTNERS Practice the conversation again.

Extension

More Practice
ActiveBook *Self-Study Disc*
grammar · vocabulary · listening
reading · speaking · pronunciation

1 3:34 ◀)) **READING** Read about where people live. Who lives in a house? Who lives in an apartment?

Where Do You Live?

Ana Karina Espinel

My name is Ana Karina Espinel. I live in Cumbaya, Ecuador. My family has a very nice house with a two-car garage. It has a big, beautiful garden.

Downstairs there is a large living room, a dining room, and a large kitchen. Upstairs there are four bedrooms. And we have a lot of bathrooms—five in all!

My mother also has an office upstairs. We love our house.

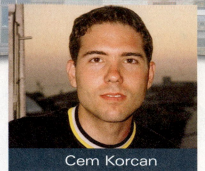

Cem Korcan

I'm Cem Korcan and I'm from Turkey. I live in a three-bedroom apartment in Istanbul. The building has a garage and a big garden.

I have one bathroom, a big living room, and a small kitchen. There's no dining room. It's a small apartment, but that's OK.

My favorite room is the living room. It has a beautiful view of Istanbul and the sea.

Soon-Ju Cho

I'm Soon-Ju Cho, from Korea. I'm a bank assistant. I live in a small house with my husband, Sun-Yoon Jong. We have three floors and a garage. There are two bedrooms, a small living room, a small kitchen, a dining room, and one bathroom.

My favorite room is the living room because it has a TV! I really want a garden, but unfortunately, we don't have one.

2 **READING COMPREHENSION** Check the descriptions that match each person's home.

	Ana Karina Espinel	Cem Korcan	Soon-Ju Cho
four bedrooms	☐	☐	☐
five bathrooms	☐	☐	☐
a small kitchen	☐	☐	☐
no dining room	☐	☐	☐
no garden	☐	☐	☐
a garage	☐	☐	☐
an office	☐	☐	☐

3 **PAIR WORK** Compare your home with the homes in the Reading.

❝ I like Ms. Espinel's house. There's a big garden. My house doesn't have a garden. ❞

❝ Mr. Korcan lives in an apartment. I live in an apartment, too. His apartment has one bathroom, but my apartment has two. ❞

On your *ActiveBook* Self-Study Disc:
Extra Reading Comprehension Questions

GRAMMAR BOOSTER
Extra practice • p. 141

3:35–3:36
Top Notch Pop
"Home Is Where the Heart Is"   Lyrics p. 148

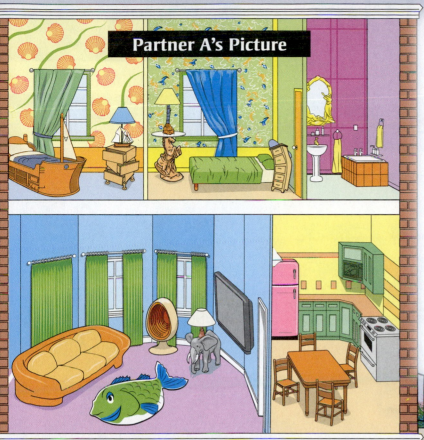

Partner A's Picture

INFO GAP Find everything that's different in the two pictures. Ask questions. For example:

How many ___ are there?   Is there ___ ?
Does the ___ have ___ ?   Are there ___ ?

PAIR WORK

1 Express your opinions about the houses, the furniture, and the appliances. For example:
A: What do you think of ___ ?
B: I think it's really nice. What about you?

2 Your partner closes his or her book. You describe one of the houses. Your partner draws a picture of the house. For example:
Upstairs, there are two small bedrooms and a small bathroom.

WRITING Compare your home with one of the houses on this page. For example:

This house has two bedrooms upstairs, but my house has . . .

Partner B's Picture

NOW I CAN...

- [ ] Describe my neighborhood.
- [ ] Ask about someone's home.
- [ ] Talk about furniture and appliances.

Activities and Plans

GOALS After Unit 9, you will be able to:
1 Describe today's weather.
2 Ask about people's activities.
3 Discuss plans.

LESSON 1

GOAL **Describe today's weather**

VOCABULARY BOOSTER
More weather vocabulary • p. 131

1 🔊 **VOCABULARY** • *Weather expressions* Read and listen. Then listen again and repeat.

3:37

HOW'S THE WEATHER?

1 It's sunny.

2 It's cloudy.

6 It's hot.

7 It's cold.

3 It's windy.

4 It's raining.

5 It's snowing.

8 It's warm.

9 It's cool.

2 🔊 **LISTENING COMPREHENSION**
3:38

Listen to the weather reports. Check the correct word for each city. Then listen again and write the temperatures. Finally, listen again and describe the weather.

City	Hot	Warm	Cool	Cold	What's the temperature?	How's the weather?
1 Cali	✓				35°	It's sunny.
2 Madrid						
3 Seoul						
4 Dubai						
5 Montreal						

3 **GRAMMAR** • *The present continuous: statements*

The present continuous expresses actions in progress now. Use a form of <u>be</u> and a present participle.

Affirmative
I**'m studying**.
You**'re shaving**.
She**'s taking** a bath.
It**'s raining**.
We**'re watching** TV.
They**'re exercising**.

Negative
I**'m not eating**.
You**'re not making** lunch. [OR You **aren't making** lunch.]
She**'s not taking** a shower. [OR She **isn't taking** a shower.]
It**'s not snowing**. [OR It **isn't snowing**.]
We**'re not reading**. [OR We **aren't reading**.]
They**'re not taking** a nap. [OR They **aren't taking** a nap.]

Present participles
wear → wearing
study → studying
exercise → exercising
Some others:
doing, listening, reading, working, meeting, getting

4 GRAMMAR • *The present continuous: <u>yes</u> / <u>no</u> questions*

Are you **eating** right now?	Yes, I am. / No, I'm not.
Is she **taking** the bus?	Yes, she is. / No, she's not. [OR No, she isn't.]
Is it **raining**?	Yes, it is. / No, it's not. [OR No, it isn't.]
Are they **walking**?	Yes, they are. / No, they're not. [OR No, they aren't.]

5 GRAMMAR PRACTICE Complete each statement, question, or short answer with the present continuous. Use contractions.

1 .... now, and .... a nice, warm sweater.
   It / snow   I / wear

2 ....? Yes, he .... his textbook.
   he /study   He / read

3 .... dinner right now. .... late at the office.
   Dad / not make   He / work

4 .... , and .... a shower.
   Jerome / exercise   Ann / take

5 .... TV. .... to music.
   The children / not watch   They / listen

6 .... this morning? No. It's cloudy and windy, but it ....
   it / rain   not rain

7 .... in the office right now? Yes, ...
   they / meet

NOW YOU CAN **Describe today's weather**

3:39
1 🔊 **CONVERSATION MODEL** Read and listen.

A: Hi, Molly. Jonathan.

B: Hey, Jonathan. Where are you?

A: I'm calling from Vancouver.
How's the weather there in São Paulo?

B: Today? Awful. It's raining and cold.

A: No kidding! It's hot and sunny here.

3:40
2 🔊 **RHYTHM AND INTONATION** Listen again and repeat. Then practice the Conversation Model with a partner.

3 PAIR WORK Change the model. Choose two cities. Role-play a conversation about the weather there. (Option: Find the weather report in the newspaper. Or log onto www.weather.com.) Then change roles.

A: Hi, ...

B: .... , ... Where are you?

A: I'm calling from ....
How's the weather there in ....?

B: Today? .... It's ....

A: No kidding! It's .... here.

4 CHANGE PARTNERS Describe the weather in other places.

bad ☹
awful
terrible

good ☺
nice
great
beautiful

a scarf

a coat

Don't stop!
Tell your partner what you're wearing.
I'm wearing ___.
I'm not wearing ___.

GOAL | **Ask about people's activities**

1 GRAMMAR • *The present continuous: information questions*

> What **is** she **wearing**? (A long black skirt.)   What **are** you **doing**? (We're checking e-mail.)
> Where **is** he **driving**? (To work.)   Where **are** they **going**? (They're going to the movies.)
>
> **BUT: Note the different word order when <u>who</u> is the subject.**
> Who **is working**? (Ben.)

2 PAIR WORK Ask and answer questions about Mike and Patty.
Use the present continuous and <u>What</u>, <u>Where</u>, and <u>Who</u>.

> 66 It's 8:20. What's Mike doing? 99
>
> 66 He's eating breakfast. 99

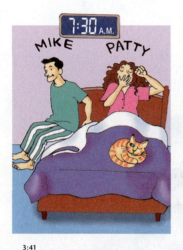

3 🔊 PRONUNCIATION • *Rising and falling intonation* Use rising intonation for <u>yes</u> / <u>no</u> questions.
Use falling intonation for information questions. Read and listen. Then listen again and repeat.

3:41

<u>Yes</u>/<u>no</u> questions	Information questions
1 Are you eating?	What are you eating?
2 Is he walking?	Where is he walking?
3 Are they watching a movie?	Who's watching a movie?
4 Is her family at home?	Where is her family?
5 Are you a teacher?	What do you do?

4 GRAMMAR • *The present participle: spelling rules*

base form		present participle	base form		present participle
talk	→	**talking**	make	→	**making**
read	→	**reading**	take	→	**taking**
watch	→	**watching**	come	→	**coming**

Remember:
shop → sho**pp**ing   get → ge**tt**ing   put → pu**tt**ing

5 GRAMMAR PRACTICE Write the present participle of each base form.

1 read .... 3 wash .... 5 drive ....

2 write .... 4 go .... 6 get up ....

6 🔊 **LISTENING COMPREHENSION** Listen. Complete each statement in the present continuous.

3:42

1 Sara's .... 4 Paul's ....

2 Dan's .... 5 Marla's ....

3 Eva's ....

NOW YOU CAN Ask about people's activities

1 🔊 **CONVERSATION MODEL** Read and listen.

3:43

A: Hello?

B: Hi, Grace. This is Jessica. What are you doing?

A: Well, actually, I'm doing the laundry right now.

B: Oh, I'm sorry. Should I call you back later?

A: Yes, thanks. Talk to you later. Bye.

B: Bye.

2 🔊 **RHYTHM AND INTONATION** Listen again and repeat. Then practice the Conversation Model with a partner.

3:44

3 PAIR WORK Role-play a telephone call. Use your own names. Use the pictures or use your own activities. Then change roles.

A: Hello?

B: Hi, ... This is .... What are you doing?

A: Well, actually, I .... right now.

B: Oh, I'm sorry. Should I call you back later?

A: Yes, thanks. Talk to you later. Bye.

B: ....

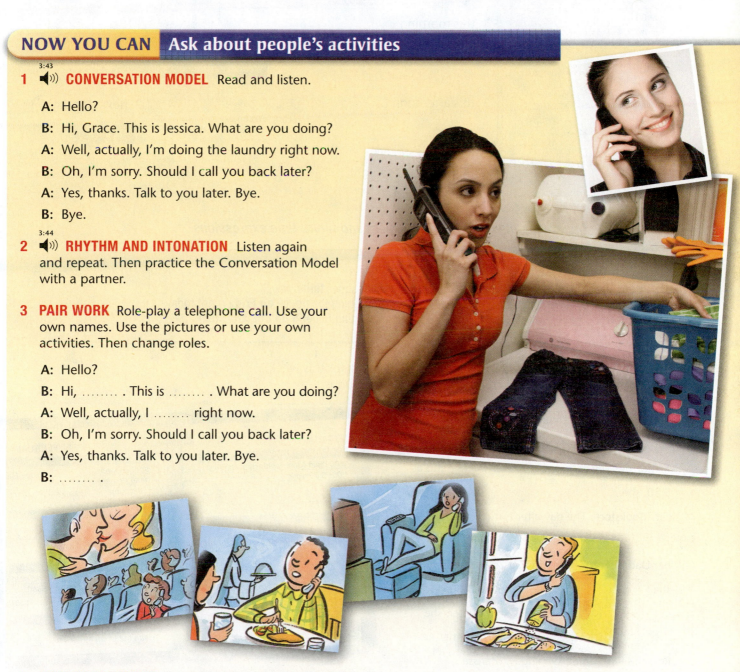

4 CHANGE PARTNERS Ask and talk about other activities.

GOAL Discuss plans

1 🔊 **VOCABULARY** • *More time expressions* Read and listen. Then listen again and repeat.

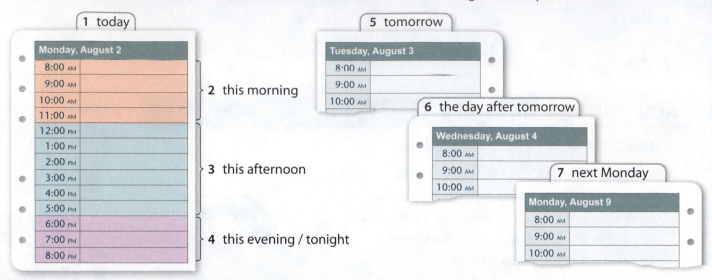

2 GRAMMAR • *The present continuous with present and future time expressions*

Actions in the present	Future plans
Are you watching TV **right now**?	I'm buying shoes **tomorrow**.
I'm not studying English **this year**.	They're cleaning the house **on Friday**, not today.
She's working at home **this week**.	Janet's meeting Bill **at 5:00 this afternoon**.

3 GRAMMAR PRACTICE Read Marissa Miller's date book for this week. Then complete the paragraph. Use the present continuous.

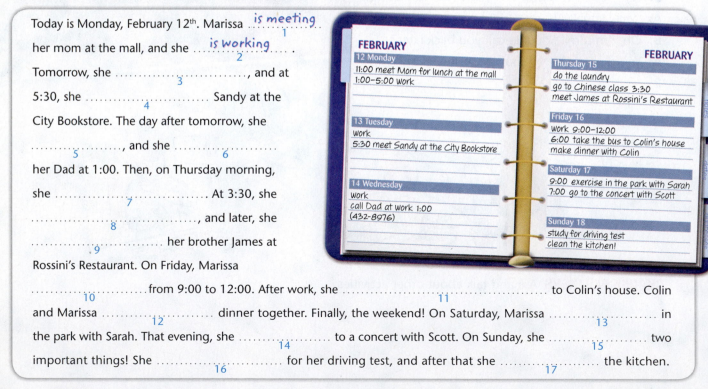

Today is Monday, February 12th. Marissa *is meeting* ....1.... her mom at the mall, and she *is working* ....2..... Tomorrow, she ....3................., and at 5:30, she ....4............... Sandy at the City Bookstore. The day after tomorrow, she ....5................, and she ....6................ her Dad at 1:00. Then, on Thursday morning, she ....7.................. At 3:30, she ....8................., and later, she ....9................. her brother James at Rossini's Restaurant. On Friday, Marissa ....10................from 9:00 to 12:00. After work, she ....11................ to Colin's house. Colin and Marissa ....12............... dinner together. Finally, the weekend! On Saturday, Marissa ....13............... in the park with Sarah. That evening, she ....14................. to a concert with Scott. On Sunday, she ....15................. two important things! She ....16................. for her driving test, and after that she ....17................. the kitchen.

4 PAIR WORK Ask your partner three <u>yes</u> / <u>no</u> questions and three information questions about Marissa's schedule. Use the present continuous. Answer your partner's questions.

> " Is Marissa exercising on Tuesday? "

> " Where is she making dinner on Friday? "

NOW YOU CAN Discuss plans

1 🔊 **CONVERSATION MODEL** Read and listen.
<small>3:46</small>

A: So what are you doing this weekend?

B: I'm not sure. What about you?

A: Well, on Saturday, if the weather is good, I'm meeting Pam in the park.

B: Do you want to get together on Sunday? I'm not doing anything special.

A: Sure! Call me Sunday morning.

2 🔊 **RHYTHM AND INTONATION** Listen again and repeat. Then practice the Conversation Model with a partner.
<small>3:47</small>

3 PLAN YOUR CONVERSATION Fill in the date book for this week. Write your activities and the times.

Monday

Tuesday

Wednesday

Thursday

Friday

Saturday

Sunday

4 PAIR WORK Use the date book to personalize the conversation with real information. Then change roles.

A: So what are you doing ....?

B: .... What about you?

A: Well, on ....

B: Do you want to get together ....? I'm not doing anything special.

A: ....! Call me ....

Don't stop!
Ask about plans for other days of the week.

♻ **Be sure to recycle this language.**

Time expressions	Weather expressions	Ways to agree
on [Friday]	raining	Sure!
this [afternoon]	snowing	OK!
in the [evening]	if it's ⎧ hot / cold	Good idea!
tomorrow	windy	
the day after tomorrow	sunny	

5 CHANGE PARTNERS Discuss other plans.

3:48

1 🔊 **READING** Read the newspaper column.

Samantha Keyes

What's going on in Compton Beach?
Around Town with Samantha Keyes

Singer Luncheonette is singing all this week at the Cadillac Café Restaurant and Concert Space. She has some great new songs, so run, don't walk, to the Cadillac Café if you want a seat for one of the weekend shows.

The French movie *I Have No Life* is playing Friday and Saturday at the Seymour Movie theater on Old Town Road, next to the Town Square Shopping Center. There are two shows: the early show starts at 8:20, and the late show is at 11:45.

Shh! Don't tell anyone, but the Elegance Hair Salon is having a special event this weekend at the Templeton Mall. Elegance usually washes and cuts hair at their salon in the Plaza Hotel, but this weekend only, they're having a half-price sale for the first 100 customers at the Templeton Mall.

On Saturday morning, Vin Blackwell, who usually teaches exercise classes for Hollywood movie stars, is speaking about exercises you can do at work, school, and the mall. Blackwell isn't very young, but he exercises morning, noon, and night. Whether you're a morning person or an evening person, he has something right for you.

2 **READING COMPREHENSION** Check the statements that are true. Correct the statements that are not true.

☐ **1** Samantha Keyes is a singer.

☐ **2** *I Have No Life* is playing at the Town Square Shopping Center.

☐ **3** Elegance Hair Salon's usual address is the Plaza Hotel.

☐ **4** Vin Blackwell is a movie star.

☐ **5** Mr. Blackwell only exercises on Saturdays.

On your *ActiveBook* Self-Study Disc:
Extra Reading Comprehension Questions

3 **GAME** Team 1 mimes an activity. Team 2 asks questions. Use the activities from the box.

comb your hair
drive
exercise
talk on the phone
get dressed
take a shower
read
watch TV

go to bed
brush your teeth
wash the dishes
take out the garbage

check e-mail
listen to music
put on makeup

Are you putting on makeup?

GRAMMAR BOOSTER
Extra practice • p.142

PAIR WORK Create telephone conversations for Sam and Debbie on Thursday and on Saturday. Ask about activities and plans. Ask about the weather. For example:

Hi, Sam. This is Debbie. I'm calling from ...

WRITING Write five sentences about your plans for next week. Use the present continuous. For example:

I'm going out for dinner on Saturday.

Review

Thursday, May 5, 1:20 p.m.

Saturday, May 7, 6:30 p.m.

NOW I CAN... ✔

☐ Describe today's weather.
☐ Ask about people's activities.
☐ Discuss plans.

79

Food

GOALS After Unit 10, you will be able to:

1 Discuss ingredients for a recipe.
2 Offer and ask for foods.
3 Invite someone to join you at the table.

LESSON 1

GOAL Discuss ingredients for a recipe

4:02

1 🔊)) **VOCABULARY** • *Foods: count nouns* Read and listen. Then listen again and repeat.

1 an egg

2 an onion

3 an apple

4 an orange

5 a lemon

6 a banana

7 a tomato

8 a potato

9 a pepper

10 beans

11 peas

VOCABULARY BOOSTER

More vegetables and fruits • p. 132

4:03

2 🔊)) **LISTENING COMPREHENSION** Listen to the conversations. Check the foods you hear in each conversation.

1		✓					✓	✓
2								
3								
4								
5								

3 **PAIR WORK** Which foods do you like? Tell your partner. Compare your likes and dislikes.

❝I don't like bananas, but I really like apples.❞

4 **GRAMMAR** • *How many / Are there any*

> Use <u>How many</u> and <u>Are there any</u> with plural nouns.
> **How many** onions **are there**?   (Ten or twelve.)
> **How many** apples **are there** in the refrigerator?   (I'm not sure. Maybe two.)
> **Are there any** lemons?   (Yes, there are.   OR   Yes. There are three.)
>   (No, there aren't. OR No. There aren't any.)

5 4:04 🔊 **VOCABULARY** • *Places to keep food in a kitchen* Read and listen. Then listen again and repeat.

1 in the fridge (in the refrigerator)   **2** on the shelf   **3** on the counter

6 **PAIR WORK** Ask and answer questions about the Vocabulary pictures. Use <u>How many</u> and <u>Are there any</u>.

❝ How many potatoes are there on the shelf? ❞

❝ There are three. ❞

NOW YOU CAN | **Discuss ingredients for a recipe**

Green Bean Salad

Ingredients:
beans
peas
onions

Fruit Salad

Ingredients:
apples
bananas
oranges

Tomato Potato Soup

Ingredients:
tomatoes
potatoes
onions

Potato Pancakes

Ingredients:
potatoes
onions
eggs

Stuffed Peppers

Ingredients:
peppers
tomatoes
onions

1 4:05 🔊 **CONVERSATION MODEL** Read and listen.

A: How about some green bean salad?

B: Green bean salad? That sounds delicious! I love green beans.

A: Are there any beans in the fridge?

B: Yes, there are.

A: And do we have any onions?

B: I'm not sure. I'll check.

2 4:06 🔊 **RHYTHM AND INTONATION** Listen again and repeat. Then practice the Conversation Model with a partner.

3 **PAIR WORK** Change the model. Use the recipes. Then change roles. Start like this:

A: How about some ....?

B: ....? That sounds delicious! I love ....

A: Are there any ....?

B: ....

Continue with the other ingredients in the recipe.

 Be sure to recycle this language.

We need ___ .	We don't have ___ .
I like ___ .	I don't like ___ .
What do you think?	
Sounds great.	

Don't stop!
Talk about what you need, want, have, and like.

4 **CHANGE PARTNERS** Discuss another recipe.

81

GOAL · Offer and ask for foods

1 🔊 4:07 **VOCABULARY** • *Drinks and foods: non-count nouns* Read and listen. Then listen again and repeat.

Drinks

1 water **2** coffee **3** tea **4** juice **5** milk **6** soda

Foods

7 bread **8** pasta **9** rice **10** cheese **11** meat **12** chicken

13 fish **14** oil **15** butter **16** sugar **17** salt **18** pepper

2 **GROUP WORK** Which foods from the Vocabulary do you like? Discuss with your classmates.

"I like cheese."

"Me too! Cheese is my favorite food!"

"Not me. I really don't like cheese."

3 **GRAMMAR** • *Count nouns and non-count nouns*

Count nouns name things you can count. They can be singular or plural.	Non-count nouns name things you can not count. They are not singular or plural.
I want an **apple**.	I don't eat **sugar**.
I like **bananas**.	**Rice** is good for you.
We have three **tomatoes** on the shelf.	**Cheese** is my favorite food.

Be careful!
- Use singular verbs with non-count nouns.
  Rice is good for you.
  NOT Rice ~~are~~ good for you.
- Don't use -s or a / an with non-count nouns.
  water NOT ~~a water~~
         NOT ~~waters~~

4 **GRAMMAR PRACTICE** Complete the chart. Be careful!
Make the count nouns plural. Then compare with a partner.

I eat	pasta, peas...
I don't eat	
I drink	
I don't drink	

5 **GRAMMAR** • *How much / Is there any*

Use **How much** to ask about non-count nouns.
How much bread does she want? (NOT ~~How many~~ bread does she want?)
How much milk is there? (NOT ~~How many~~ milk is there?)
Is there any butter? Yes, there is. / No, there isn't. OR No. There isn't any.

Remember:
Use **How many** with plural count nouns.
How many apples are there?
NOT ~~How much~~ apples are there?

4:08
6 🔊 **VOCABULARY** • *Containers and quantities* Read and listen. Then listen again and repeat.

1 a box of pasta   2 a loaf of bread   3 a bottle of juice   4 a can of soda   5 a bag of onions

7 **GRAMMAR PRACTICE** Complete each question with **How much** or **How many**.

1 .... loaves of bread do you need?

2 .... bags of potatoes do we have?

3 .... cheese is there in the fridge?

4 .... sugar do you want in your tea?

5 .... eggs are there for the potato pancakes?

6 .... cans of tomatoes are there on the shelf?

NOW YOU CAN | **Offer and ask for foods**

4:09
1 🔊 **CONVERSATION MODEL** Read and listen.

A: Would you like coffee or tea?

B: I'd like coffee, please. Thanks.

A: And would you like sugar?

B: No, thanks.

A: Please pass the butter.

B: Here you go.

4:10
2 🔊 **RHYTHM AND INTONATION**
Listen again and repeat. Then practice
the Conversation Model with a partner.

3 **PAIR WORK** Change the model. Use other
foods and drinks. Then change roles.

A: Would you like .... or ....?

B: I'd like ...., please. Thanks.

A: And would you like ....?

B: ....

A: Please pass the ....

B: Here you go.

Don't stop!
Offer other foods and
drinks.

4 **CHANGE PARTNERS** Change the model again.

GOAL Invite someone to join you at the table

1 GRAMMAR • *The simple present tense and the present continuous*

Remember: Use the simple present tense with verbs <u>have</u>, <u>want</u>, <u>need</u>, and <u>like</u>.

I **like** coffee. NOT ~~I'm liking~~ coffee.

Use the simple present tense to describe habitual actions and with frequency adverbs.

I **cook** dinner every day.
I never **eat** eggs for breakfast.

Use the present continuous for actions in progress right now.

We**'re making** dinner now.
She**'s studying** English this year.

Be careful!
Don't say: We ~~cook~~ dinner now.
Don't say: I ~~am cooking~~ dinner every day.

2 GRAMMAR PRACTICE Complete each statement or question with the simple present tense or the present continuous.

1 Who .... lunch in the kitchen right now?
     eat

2 Where .... he usually .... lunch—at
     home or at the office?   *eat*

3 They .... a lot of sugar in their tea.
          not like

4 We .... the kitchen every day.
          clean

5 Elaine and Joe aren't here. They ....
     to work.   *drive*

6 Why .... six cans of tomatoes?
          you / need
     .... tomato soup for lunch?
          make

7 .... to work tomorrow?
          you / go

8 How many boxes of rice ....?
                    you / want

9 I .... a bottle of juice in the fridge.
        not have

10 I can't talk right now. I ....
                    study

3 GRAMMAR PRACTICE Look at Suzanne and her weekly schedule. On a separate sheet of paper, write about Suzanne. What is she doing right now? What does she do at other times? Use the present continuous and the simple present tense.

May

10 Monday
Teach English [intermediate]
     at Linguatec: 10:00 A.M.

11 Tuesday
Work at home 8:00–12:00
Teach English [beginning] at Bank
     Street School: 4:00–6:00

12 Wednesday
Teach English [intermediate]
     at Linguatec: 10:00 A.M.

May

Thursday 13
Work at home 8:00–12:00
Teach English [beginning] at Bank
     Street School: 4:00–6:00

Friday 14
Study Chinese

Saturday 15
Laundry / shopping

Sunday 16
Cook for Mom and Dad

Suzanne is listening to music right now. She teaches English on Mondays and...

4 PAIR WORK Ask and answer questions about Suzanne's activities. Use the simple present tense and the present continuous.

❝ What's Suzanne doing right now? ❞

❝ She's listening to music. ❞

❝ Does Suzanne teach English? ❞

❝ Yes, she does. ❞

5 🔊 **PRONUNCIATION** • *Vowel sounds* Read and listen. Then listen again and repeat.

1 /i/	2 /ɪ/	3 /eɪ/	4 /ɛ/	5 /æ/
see	six	late	pepper	apple
tea	fish	potato	red	jacket
street	this	train	lemon	has

6 PAIR WORK Read a word from Pronunciation aloud. On a separate sheet of paper, your partner writes the word.

NOW YOU CAN **Invite someone to join you at the table**

1 🔊 **CONVERSATION MODEL** Read and listen.
4:12

A: Hi, Alison. Nice to see you!

B: You too, Rita. Do you come here often?

A: Yes, I do. Would you like to join me?

B: Sure. What are you drinking?

A: Lemonade.

B: Mmm. Sounds good.

2 🔊 **RHYTHM AND INTONATION** Listen again and repeat. Then practice the Conversation Model with a partner.
4:13

3 PAIR WORK Change the model. Use your own name and your own foods or drinks or use the pictures. Then change roles.

A: Hi, ... Nice to see you!

B: You too, ... Do you come here often?

A: Yes, I do. Would you like to join me?

B: .... What are you ....?

A: ....

B: Mmm. Sounds good.

Don't stop!
Offer other foods and drinks

♻ **Be sure to recycle this language.**

Would you like ___ ?
Sure. / No thanks.

4 CHANGE PARTNERS Invite another classmate to join you.

Extension

More Practice
ActiveBook Self-Study Disc
grammar • vocabulary • listening
reading • speaking • pronunciation

4:14
1 READING Read a recipe with only three ingredients.

Hungarian Cabbage and Noodles

Ingredients

1 large head of green cabbage
1/2 cup unsalted butter
11 ounces (700 grams) of egg noodles

1. Cut the cabbage into small slices.
2. Put the cabbage into a large bowl and add salt.
3. Put the cabbage into the refrigerator overnight.
4. The next day, drain the cabbage.
5. Melt the butter in a large pan.
6. Sauté the cabbage until it is light brown and very soft (30-40 minutes).
7. Cook the noodles and drain them. Mix them with the cabbage. Add lots of black pepper.

Source: Adapted from *Recipes 1-2-3* by Rozanne Gold (New York: Viking, 1997)

4:15
Cooking verbs

2 READING COMPREHENSION Answer the questions.

1 How many ingredients does the recipe have?
2 What are the ingredients?
3 Is there any butter or oil in the recipe?

4:16
3 LISTENING COMPREHENSION Listen to the radio cooking program. Write the correct quantity next to each ingredient. Then listen again and number the pictures in the correct order. Listen again and check your work.

On your *ActiveBook* Self-Study Disc:
Extra Reading Comprehension Questions

Pasta with Garlic and Olive Oil

Ingredients:

__ cloves of garlic
__ tablespoons of olive oil
__ box of pasta

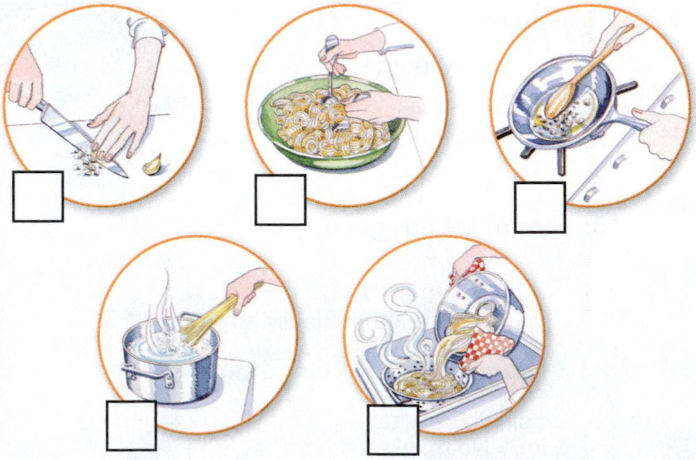

4 SPEAKING PRACTICE Tell a partner what you eat for each meal.

"My favorite food for breakfast is eggs."

GRAMMAR BOOSTER
Extra practice • p. 143

4:17/4:18
Top Notch Pop
"Fruit Salad, Baby" Lyrics p. 148

Monday

Monday /Wednesday / Friday
Michael: do laundry
                    (Monday only)
Sylvia: go shopping
Sylvia: cook dinner

Tuesday / Thursday / Saturday
Sylvia: take out the garbage
Michael: go shopping and cook
                    dinner

Sunday
No Chores!

MEMORY GAME Look at the pictures for one minute. Then close your books and say all the foods and drinks you remember. Use count and non-count nouns correctly.

PAIR WORK

1 Ask and answer questions about the pictures. Use <u>How many</u> and <u>How much</u>. Answer with <u>There is</u> and <u>There are</u>. For example:

A: How many boxes of pasta are there on the counter?
B: There are two.

2 Create conversations for Michael and Sylvia in the three pictures. For example:

A: Would you like peas?
B: Yes, please. And please pass the salt.

DESCRIPTION Describe the activities and habitual actions. Use the present continuous and the simple present tense. For example:

It's Tuesday. Michael is cooking dinner. Sylvia cooks dinner on Monday.

WRITING Write about what you eat in a typical day. Start like this:

For breakfast I eat...

Tuesday

Friday

NOW I CAN... ✔

☐ Discuss ingredients for a recipe.
☐ Offer and ask for foods.
☐ Invite someone to join me at the table.

Past Events

LESSON 1

GOAL   Tell someone about a past event

1 🔊 **VOCABULARY** • *Describing times before today* Read and listen. Then listen again and repeat.

1 the day before yesterday — August 30
2 yesterday — August 31
today — September 1

3 last { week / month / year / Tuesday } today

4 two { days / weeks / months / years } ago   today

🔊 Years, decades, and centuries
1900 = nineteen hundred
1901 = nineteen oh one
2001 = two thousand one
2010 = two thousand ten / twenty ten
1990 to 1999 = the (nineteen) nineties
1901 to 2000 = the twentieth century
2001 to 2100 = the twenty-first century

2 🔊 **LISTENING COMPREHENSION** Listen and circle the year you hear.

1 1913 / 1930   3 1967 / 1976
2 2016 / 2060   4 2001 / 2021

3 **PAIR WORK** Choose five of the following years. Say a year to your partner. Your partner circles the year.

2008 **1914** **1910** **1809** **1955** **1800**
1998 **1814** **1615** **2016** **1922** **2012**

4 **GRAMMAR** • *The past tense of be*

I / He / She { was / wasn't } at school yesterday.

We / You / They { were / weren't } at home.

Contractions
was not → wasn't
were not → weren't

It was cloudy yesterday.
There was a concert last night.
There were two movies last weekend.

Was he at work yesterday?
Where **was the party** last night?
When **was she** in Italy?

Were they students in the eighties?
Where **were they** last weekend?
When **were you** at the bookstore?

BUT: When <u>who</u> is the subject:
Who was at the party? (Adam was.)

5 GRAMMAR PRACTICE With a partner, take turns asking and answering the questions about the calendar. Today is April 20.

1 What day was yesterday?   **"** Yesterday was April 19th. **"**

2 What day was six days ago?

3 What day was one month ago?

4 What day was the day before yesterday?

5 What were the dates of last Saturday and Sunday?

6 What day was two months ago?

APRIL

Sun	Mon	Tues	Wed	Thurs	Fri	Sat
	1	2	3	4	5	6
7	8	9	10	11	12	13
14	15	16	17	18	19	**20**
21	22	23	24	25	26	27
28	29	30				

4:22

6 📢)) LISTENING COMPREHENSION Listen to the conversations about events. Then listen again and circle the correct day or month.

1 If today is Sunday, then the party was on (Saturday / Friday / Thursday).

2 If this is January, then their birthdays were in (February / December / January).

3 If today is Friday, then the game was on (Monday / Thursday / Wednesday).

NOW YOU CAN   **Tell someone about a past event**

4:23

1 📢)) CONVERSATION MODEL Read and listen.

A: Where were you last night?

B: What time?

A: At about 8:00.

B: I was at home. Why?

A: Because there was a great party at Celia's house.

B: There was? Too bad I wasn't there!

4:24

2 📢)) RHYTHM AND INTONATION Listen again and repeat. Then practice the Conversation Model with a partner.

3 PAIR WORK Make a list of places for an event in your town. Or use the pictures of events. Then change the model. Then change roles.

A: Where were you ....?

B: What time?

A: At about ....

B: I was at .... Why?

A: Because there was .... at ....

B: There was? Too bad I wasn't there!

4 CHANGE PARTNERS Talk about other events and places.

GOAL   Describe past activities

1 GRAMMAR • *The simple past tense*

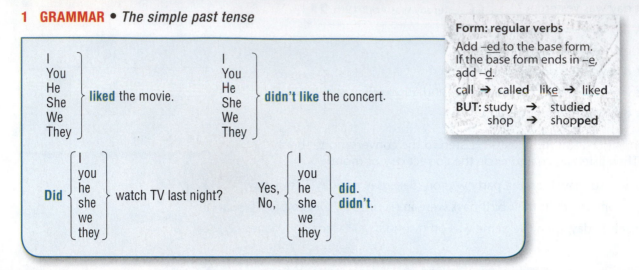

Form: regular verbs

Add –<u>ed</u> to the base form.
If the base form ends in –<u>e</u>,
add –<u>d</u>.

call → call**ed**   like → lik**ed**

BUT: study → stud**ied**
shop → shop**ped**

I / You / He / She / We / They **liked** the movie.

I / You / He / She / We / They **didn't like** the concert.

Did I / you / he / she / we / they watch TV last night?

Yes, I / you / he / she / we / they **did**.
No, I / you / he / she / we / they **didn't**.

2 GRAMMAR PRACTICE Complete the e-mail. Use the simple past tense and the past tense of <u>be</u>.

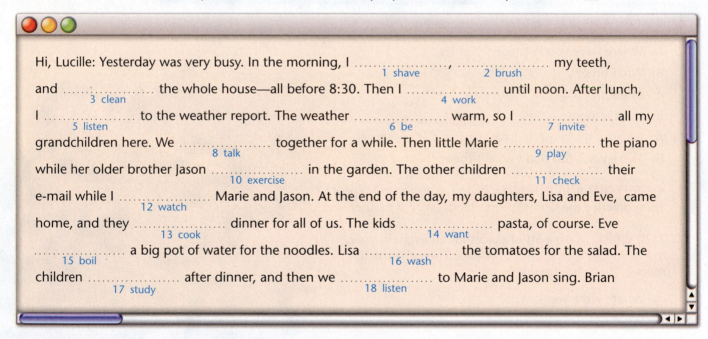

Hi, Lucille: Yesterday was very busy. In the morning, I ...., ... my teeth,
                              1 shave   2 brush

and .... the whole house—all before 8:30. Then I .... until noon. After lunch,
    3 clean   4 work

I .... to the weather report. The weather .... warm, so I .... all my
  5 listen   6 be   7 invite

grandchildren here. We .... together for a while. Then little Marie .... the piano
            8 talk   9 play

while her older brother Jason .... in the garden. The other children .... their
                 10 exercise   11 check

e-mail while I .... Marie and Jason. At the end of the day, my daughters, Lisa and Eve, came
       12 watch

home, and they .... dinner for all of us. The kids .... pasta, of course. Eve
        13 cook   14 want

.... a big pot of water for the noodles. Lisa .... the tomatoes for the salad. The
  15 boil   16 wash

children .... after dinner, and then we .... to Marie and Jason sing. Brian
       17 study   18 listen

3 GRAMMAR • *The simple past tense: information questions*

What **did** you **do** last weekend?
Where **did** you **go**?
When **did** he **get** home last night?
How many cups of coffee **did** she **drink**?
How often **did** you **take** a nap?
Who **did** they **see** yesterday?

BUT: The word order changes when <u>Who</u> is the subject:

Who went to the mall this morning? (We did.)

4:25
🔊 **Irregular verbs** (Also see page 125.)

buy →	bought	eat →	ate	read →	read
come →	came	get →	got	say →	said
cut →	cut	go →	went	see →	saw
do →	did	have →	had	take →	took
drink →	drank	make →	made	think →	thought
drive →	drove	put →	put	write →	wrote

4 🔊 **PRONUNCIATION • *The simple past tense ending*** Listen. Then listen again and repeat.

1 /d/	**2** /t/	**3** /ɪd/
listened = listen/d/	liked = like/t/	wanted = want/ɪd/
exercised = exercise/d/	washed = wash/t/	needed = need/ɪd/

5 🔊 **GRAMMAR PRACTICE** Complete the conversations. Use verbs in the simple past tense.

Conversation 1

A: Where .... on Saturday?
   1 your family / go
B: .... to the movies. ....
   _2 We / go_   _3 we / see_
   a good family movie.
A: .... out to eat afterwards?
   4 you / go
B: Yes, we .... Indonesian
   _5_   _6 We / eat_
   food. .... a lot of pepper.
   7 It / have
A: But ....
   8 I / think   _9 your husband / not like_
   peppery food.
B: He doesn't usually like peppery food, but
   .... a little. Actually, ... he
   10 he / eat   _11 he / say_
   really likes Indonesian food.

Conversation 2

A: .... out the garbage this morning?
   12 Who / take
B: Actually, Laura ....
                    _13_
A: And .... the laundry?
       14 who / do
B: I'm not sure. But I think .... the
                          15 Laura / do
   laundry this morning, too.
A: That's great, but .... any household
                    16 you / do
   chores?
B: Me? Last week .... all the chores:
                 _17 I / do_
   .... shopping, and .... home
   _18 I / go_   _19 I / come_
   early, and .... dinner every night.
              20 I / make

NOW YOU CAN **Describe past activities**

1 🔊 **CONVERSATION MODEL** Read and listen.

A: So what did you do yesterday?

B: Well, I got up at seven, I made breakfast, and then I went to work.

A: What about after work? Did you do anything special?

B: Not really. I just made dinner and watched a movie.

2 🔊 **RHYTHM AND INTONATION** Listen again and repeat. Then practice the Conversation Model with a partner.

3 **PAIR WORK** Personalize the conversation. Describe your past activities. Then change roles.

A: So what did you do ....?

B: Well, I ...., and then I ....

A: What about ....? Did you do anything special?

B: ....

Don't stop! Ask more questions.
Did you [do the dishes]?
Who [took out the garbage]?
When did you [go to the movies]?

4 **CHANGE PARTNERS** Ask about other past activities.

Ideas
• household chores
• leisure activities
• entertainment events

GOAL **Talk about outdoor activities**

VOCABULARY BOOSTER
More outdoor activities • p. 133

1 4:29 🔊 **VOCABULARY • *Outdoor activities*** Read and listen. Then listen again and repeat.

1 go to the beach

2 go running

3 go bike riding

4 go for a walk

5 go swimming

6 go for a drive

2 **PAIR WORK** Ask and answer questions with <u>When</u> and <u>How often</u> and the Vocabulary.

❝How often do you go to the beach?❞

3 4:30 🔊 **LISTENING COMPREHENSION** Listen to the conversations. Then check the correct picture to complete each statement.

1 Rosalie went ___ .

a

b

2 She's going ___ .

a

b

3 They're going ___ .

a

b

4 He went ___ .

a

b

1 🔊 4:31 **CONVERSATION MODEL** Read and listen.

A: Did you have a good weekend?

B: Let me think. . . . Oh, yeah. We had a great weekend.

A: What did you do?

B: Well, on Saturday we went bike riding and to a movie. Then on Sunday, we went for a drive. What about you?

A: Well, the weather was great, so we went for a walk on Saturday. And on Sunday we went to the beach.

2 🔊 4:32 **RHYTHM AND INTONATION** Listen again and repeat. Then practice the Conversation Model with a partner.

3 **NOTEPADDING** On the notepad, write what you did on the weekend.

On Saturday
On Sunday

4 **PAIR WORK** Personalize the conversation. Use your own information.

A: Did you have a good weekend?

B: Let me think. . . . .

A: What did you do?

B: Well, ... Then .... What about you?

A: Well, the weather was ...., so we .... on Saturday. And on Sunday we ....

5 **CHANGE PARTNERS** Talk about more activities.

Don't stop!
Ask your partner more questions in the simple past tense. Ask about other times in the past.

 Be sure to recycle this language.

Past-time expressions	Adjectives
last week	good
yesterday	nice
the day before yesterday	great
last month	bad
last [Wednesday]	awful
a [week] ago	terrible

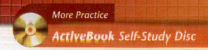

More Practice
ActiveBook Self-Study Disc
grammar · vocabulary · listening
reading · speaking · pronunciation

1 ◀)) **READING** Read about what people did last weekend.

FaceTime | Inbox | Home | Account |

Rafaela   **Mexico**

That's a picture of my husband and me. We live in Mérida, on the Yucatán Peninsula. Last weekend we drove to the small port city of Sisal. The drive wasn't very long—it took only about one hour. In Sisal, we went to the beautiful beach. We ate fish at a wonderful outdoor restaurant. The weather was beautiful—warm and sunny. We went to bed early and got up early. We had a REALLY great time. Last weekend was my favorite weekend ever!

| Comment |

Jeremy   **Jamaica**

Last weekend was awful! I went to New York because my mom and dad live there. I wanted to go to a concert and eat at a couple of good restaurants. But the weather was really bad—it rained, and it was so windy! There were no taxis, so we stayed in my parents' apartment and cooked and ate. The food was good, but it wasn't what we wanted. We watched old movies on TV. We didn't go to a concert. Next time, my parents are coming to Jamaica. It's always sunny here!

| Comment |

Clifford   **Canada**

Well, I actually had a good time. My friends came to visit me on Friday, and we went out to eat at a terrific restaurant. On Saturday, I went for a walk alone in the park, and that evening, I went dancing at a really nice nightclub with my girlfriend. (We took the picture at the nightclub.) We stayed out really late—so late that we ate breakfast when we left the nightclub. Sunday? On Sunday, I slept all day.

| Comment |

2 **READING COMPREHENSION** Write one <u>yes</u>/<u>no</u> question and one information question about Rafaela, Jeremy, and Clifford. Then answer a partner's questions.

On your *ActiveBook* Self-Study Disc:
Extra Reading Comprehension Questions

	<u>Yes</u> / <u>no</u> questions	Information questions
Rafaela		
Jeremy		
Clifford		

GRAMMAR BOOSTER

Extra practice • p. 144

Ideas
Where were you (or Where did you go) last ___ ?
What did you do?
Who were you with?
When ___ ?
What ___ ?

3 **SPEAKING PRACTICE** Ask your partner questions about an activity in the past. Then tell your classmates about the activity. Use past-time expressions.

4:34–4:35
Top Notch Pop
"My Favorite Day"   Lyrics p. 148

VERB GAME Form two teams. Look at the pictures for one minute. Then close your books. Each team makes a list of all the actions in the pictures. The team with the most actions wins. For example:
watch TV   do the laundry

STORY Tell a story about one of the people. Use past-time expressions. For example:
Last weekend, Karen went to a concert with her friends. She . . .

PAIR WORK With a partner, play the role of Don or Karen. Discuss your activities from the day before and the weekend before. Start like this:
So what did you do [last weekend?] . . .

WRITING Choose one of the following topics:
a Write about Don and Karen. Write about what they did.
b Write about your weekend. Write about what you did.
For example:
Last weekend I went to the beach . . .

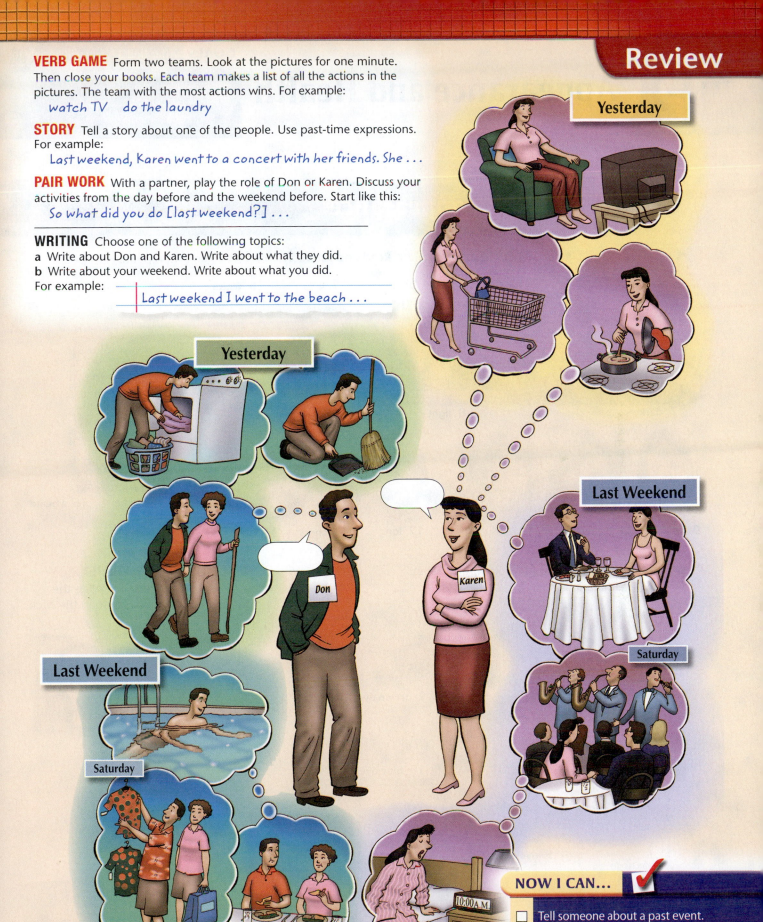

Yesterday

Yesterday

Last Weekend

Saturday

Last Weekend

Saturday

Don

Karen

Sunday

Sunday

NOW I CAN... ✔
☐ Tell someone about a past event.
☐ Describe past activities.
☐ Talk about outdoor activities.

95

Appearance and Health

GOALS After Unit 12, you will be able to:
1 Describe appearance.
2 Show concern about an injury.
3 Suggest a remedy.

LESSON 1

GOAL Describe appearance

1 ◀)) 4:36 **VOCABULARY** • *Adjectives to describe hair* Read and listen. Then listen again and repeat.

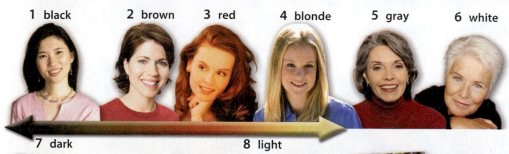

| 1 black | 2 brown | 3 red | 4 blonde | 5 gray | 6 white |

7 dark   8 light

9 straight   10 wavy   11 curly   12 long   13 short   14 bald

15 a mustache   16 a beard

2 ◀)) 4:37 **VOCABULARY** • *The face* Read and listen. Then listen again and repeat.

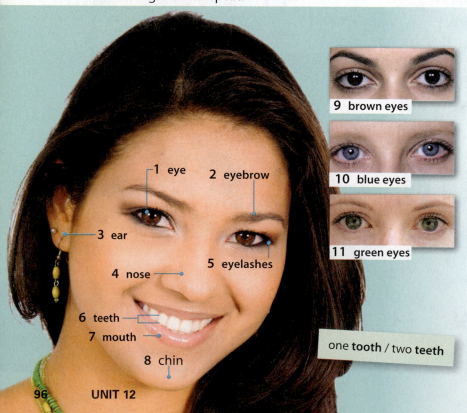

1 eye   2 eyebrow
3 ear
5 eyelashes
4 nose
6 teeth
7 mouth
8 chin

9 brown eyes

10 blue eyes

11 green eyes

one **tooth** / two **teeth**

3 ◀)) 4:38 **LISTENING COMPREHENSION** Listen to the descriptions. Write the number of the conversation in the circle.

5 GRAMMAR • *Describing people with* <u>be</u> *and* <u>have</u>

With be	**With have**
Her **eyes** are **blue**.	She has **blue eyes**.
Their **hair** is **gray**.	They have **gray hair**.
Her **eyelashes** are **long and dark**.	She has **long, dark eyelashes**.

Remember:

Adjectives come before the nouns they describe.
She has blue eyes. NOT She has ~~eyes blue~~.

Adjectives are never plural.
She has blue eyes. NOT She has ~~blues~~ eyes.
Her eyes are blue. NOT Her eyes are ~~blues~~.

6 GRAMMAR PRACTICE Complete each sentence with the correct form of <u>be</u> or <u>have</u>.

1 A: What does your brother look like?

B: Well, he .... a mustache and wavy hair.

2 A: What does your mother look like?

B: Her hair .... curly and black.

3 A: What does her father look like?

B: He .... a short, gray beard.

4 A: What does his grandmother look like?

B: She .... curly, gray hair and beautiful eyes.

5 A: What does his sister look like?

B: His sister? Her hair .... long and pretty!

6 A: What do your brothers look like?

B: They .... straight, black hair.

NOW YOU CAN Describe appearance

1 🔊 4:39 **CONVERSATION MODEL** Read and listen.

A: Who's that? She looks familiar.

B: Who?

A: The woman with the long, dark hair.

B: Oh, that's Ivete Sangalo. She's a singer from Brazil.

A: No kidding!

2 🔊 4:40 **RHYTHM AND INTONATION** Listen again and repeat. Then practice the Conversation Model with a partner.

3 **PAIR WORK** Talk about the people in the photos. (OR use your own photos.) Then change roles.

A: Who's that? .... looks familiar.

B: Who?

A: The .... with the ....

B: Oh, that's ....'s .... from ....

A: No kidding!

4 **CHANGE PARTNERS** Talk about other people.

Ivete Sangalo • singer (Brazil)

Andrea Bocelli • singer (Italy)

Gérard Depardieu • actor (France)

I. M. Pei • architect (China)

Julia Roberts • actress (the U.S.)

GOAL Show concern about an injury

1 🔊 4:41 **VOCABULARY** • *Parts of the body* Read and listen. Then listen again and repeat.

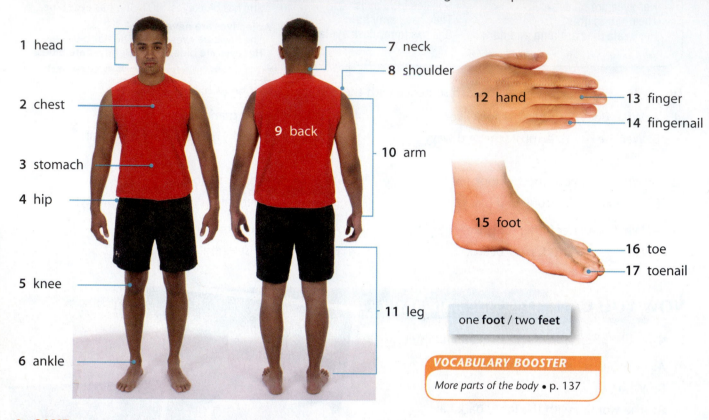

1 head
2 chest
3 stomach
4 hip
5 knee
6 ankle
7 neck
8 shoulder
9 back
10 arm
11 leg
12 hand
13 finger
14 fingernail
15 foot
16 toe
17 toenail

one **foot** / two **feet**

VOCABULARY BOOSTER
More parts of the body • p. 137

2 GAME Follow a classmate's directions. If you make a mistake, sit down.

Touch your toes.

3 🔊 4:42 **VOCABULARY** • *Accidents and injuries* Read and listen. Then listen again and repeat.

🔊 4:43

base form		past form
burn	→	burned
hurt	→	hurt
cut	→	cut
break	→	broke
fall	→	fell

1 He **burned** his finger.
2 She **hurt** her back.
3 She **cut** her hand.
4 He **broke** his arm.
5 He **fell** down.

4 ◀))） **LISTENING COMPREHENSION** Listen to the conversations. Write each injury.
Then listen again and check your work.

1 She *burned her arm* . . . .   **4** He . . . .

2 He . . . .   **5** She . . . .

3 She . . . .   **6** He . . . .

5 ◀))） **PRONUNCIATION** • *More vowel sounds* Read and listen. Then listen again and repeat.
Then practice saying the words on your own.

1 /u/	**2** /ʊ/	**3** /oʊ/	**4** /ɔ/	**5** /ɑ/
tooth	should	nose	awful	blonde
blue	good	toe	fall	hot
food	foot	broke	long	wash

NOW YOU CAN   Show concern about an injury

4:48
◀))） **Ways to express concern**
I'm sorry to hear that.
Oh, no.
That's too bad.

1 ◀))） **CONVERSATION MODEL** Read and listen.

A: Hey, Evan. What happened?

B: I broke my ankle.

A: I'm sorry to hear that. Does it hurt?

B: Actually, no. It doesn't.

2 ◀))） **RHYTHM AND INTONATION** Listen again and
repeat. Then practice the Conversation Model
with a partner.

3 **PAIR WORK** Change the model. Use the pictures
for ideas. Then change roles.

A: Hey, ... What happened?

B: I . . . .

A: . . . . Does it hurt?

B: Actually, ... It . . . .

4 **CHANGE PARTNERS** Discuss other injuries.

GOAL · Suggest a remedy

1 🔊 4:49 **VOCABULARY** · *Ailments* Read and listen. Then listen again and repeat.

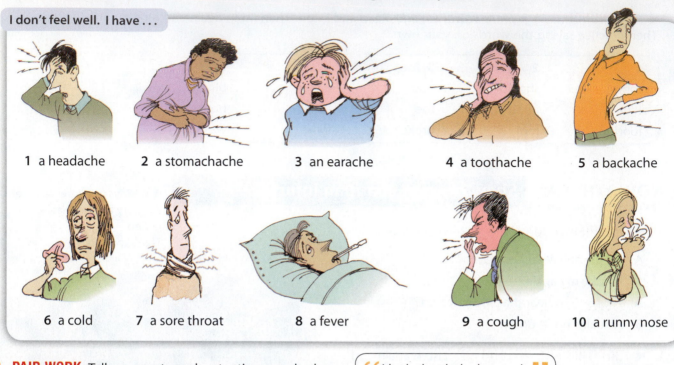

I don't feel well. I have . . .

1 a headache 2 a stomachache 3 an earache 4 a toothache 5 a backache

6 a cold 7 a sore throat 8 a fever 9 a cough 10 a runny nose

2 **PAIR WORK** Tell your partner about a time you had an ailment. Use the Vocabulary.

❝ I had a headache last week. **❞**

❝ Really? I never have headaches. **❞**

3 🔊 4:50 **VOCABULARY** · *Remedies* Read and listen. Then listen again and repeat.

1 take something 2 lie down 3 have some tea 4 see a doctor / a dentist

4 **GRAMMAR** · *Should + base form for advice*

Use **should** with the base form of a verb.

I
You
He
She
We
They
} **should take** something.
shouldn't go to work.

You **should see** a doctor.

He **shouldn't go** to school today.

5 🔊 **LISTENING COMPREHENSION** Listen to the conversations. Check the ailment. Then write the remedy. Use <u>should</u> or <u>shouldn't</u>.

	a cold	a fever	a headache	a stomachache	a sore throat	a backache	a toothache	
1	☐	☐	☐	☐	☐	☐	☐	She *should take something.*
2	☐	☐	☐	☐	☐	☐	☐	He
3	☐	☐	☐	☐	☐	☐	☐	She
4	☐	☐	☐	☐	☐	☐	☐	He
5	☐	☐	☐	☐	☐	☐	☐	She
6	☐	☐	☐	☐	☐	☐	☐	He

6 **GRAMMAR PRACTICE** Partner A: Read items 1–3. Partner B, suggest a remedy. Partner B: Read items 4–6. Partner A, suggest a remedy. Use <u>should</u> or <u>shouldn't</u>.

1 I have a backache.

2 I don't feel well. I think I have a fever.

3 My son doesn't feel well. He has a cough.

4 I have a bad toothache.

5 I have a sore throat.

6 My wife feels really bad. She has a stomachache.

NOW YOU CAN **Suggest a remedy**

1 🔊 **CONVERSATION MODEL** Read and listen.

A: I don't feel well.

B: What's wrong?

A: I have a headache.

B: Oh, that's too bad. You really should take something.

A: Good idea. Thanks.

B: I hope you feel better.

4:54
🔊 **Ways to say you're sick**
I don't feel well.
I feel terrible.
I don't feel so good.

2 🔊 **RHYTHM AND INTONATION** Listen again and repeat. Then practice the Conversation Model with a partner.

3 **PAIR WORK** Personalize the model. Then change roles.

A: ....

B: What's wrong?

A: ....

B: .... You really ....

A: .... Thanks.

B: I hope you feel better.

Don't stop! Give other advice, using <u>should</u> or <u>shouldn't</u>.
Ideas
go to bed   go to class
take a nap   exercise

4 **CHANGE PARTNERS** Discuss other ailments.

4:55

1 🔊 **READING** Look at the photos and read the descriptions. Do you know these famous people?

Shakira

Shakira Isabel Mebarak Ripoll is a singer and songwriter from Barranquilla, Colombia. Her father's family came from Lebanon, so she often listened and danced to traditional Arabic music. In 1995, at the age of 22, Shakira's Spanish-language album *Pies Descalzos* made her famous all over Latin America and Spain, and she became a star. In 2001, she recorded her first songs in English on the album *Laundry Service*. Today, Shakira is famous all over the world. Shakira was always beautiful, with long, straight, black hair. In 2001, she changed her hair style to long, curly, and blonde. But her fans love her in any hair style.

Brad Pitt

William Bradley Pitt is an actor from the U.S., famous as "Brad Pitt." He and the actress Angelina Jolie have six children. In 1985, Brad Pitt moved to Los Angeles to study acting. He began acting on TV in 1987, but soon after, he became famous in movies. With his short, straight, blonde hair and blue eyes, many people think he is very handsome. But when he isn't acting and he wants to relax, he sometimes grows his hair long. Or he doesn't shave and wears a beard. Then he doesn't look familiar to people—they don't know he's Brad Pitt, the actor.

2 READING COMPREHENSION Answer the questions.

1 Who sings in Spanish and English? ....
2 Who has six children? ....
3 Who is from Lebanon? ....
4 Where is Shakira from? ....
5 What color are Brad Pitt's eyes? ....
6 What does Pitt do when he isn't acting? ....

3 PAIR WORK Partner A describes Shakira in her two pictures. Partner B describes Brad Pitt in his two pictures. Which pictures do you like?

❝ In the first picture, Shakira has... ❞

On your *ActiveBook* Self-Study Disc:
Extra Reading Comprehension Questions

4 DISCUSSION What kind of hair is good-looking for women? What kind of hair is good-looking for men?

❝ I like long, wavy hair on women. ❞

5 GROUP WORK Describe someone in your class. Your classmates guess who it is.

❝ She's short and very good-looking. She has long hair and brown eyes. She's wearing a white blouse and a blue skirt. ❞

GRAMMAR BOOSTER

Extra practice • p. 144

GAME Play in groups of three. Partner A: Describe a person's ailment or injury. Partners B and C: Who can point to the picture first? For example:

He has a headache.

PAIR WORK

1 Describe a person. Your partner points to the picture. For example:

He has brown hair.

2 Suggest a remedy. Your partner points to the picture. For example:

She should see a doctor.

3 Create a conversation for each situation. Start like this: *I feel terrible.* OR *What happened?*

WRITING Describe someone you know. Use the vocabulary from this unit and from Unit 4. For example:

> *My friend Sue is very pretty. She has*
>
> *short, curly hair . . .*

NOW I CAN... ✓

☐ Describe appearance.
☐ Show concern about an injury.
☐ Suggest a remedy.

Abilities and Requests

GOALS After Unit 13, you will be able to:

1 Express a wish.
2 Politely decline an invitation.
3 Ask for and agree to do a favor.

LESSON 1

GOAL | Express a wish

1 5:02 🔊 **VOCABULARY** • *Abilities* Read and listen. Then listen again and repeat.

5:03 🔊 **Adverbs <u>well</u> and <u>badly</u>**

Tom **sings well.** Ryan **sings badly.**

1 sing

2 dance

3 play the guitar / the violin

4 swim

5 ski

6 cook

7 sew

8 knit

9 draw

10 paint

11 drive

12 fix things

VOCABULARY BOOSTER

More musical instruments • p. 134

2 INTEGRATED PRACTICE Write three things you do well and three things you do badly.

> **1** I sing well. I dance badly.

1		4	
2		5	
3		6	

3 PAIR WORK Tell your partner about your abilities. Use <u>well</u> and <u>badly</u>.

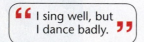
❝ I sing well, but I dance badly. ❞

4 GROUP WORK Tell your class about some of your partner's abilities.

❝ Ann sings well, but she dances badly. ❞

5 GRAMMAR • *Can* and *can't* for ability

To talk about ability, use <u>can</u> or <u>can't</u> and the base form of a verb.

She **can play** the guitar.

He **can't cook**.

Questions
Can you **play** the guitar?
Can he **speak** English?

Short answers
Yes, I **can**. / No, I **can't**.
Yes, he **can**. / No, he **can't**.

Use <u>can</u> or <u>can't</u> with <u>well</u> to indicate degree of ability.
She can play the guitar, but she can't play **well**.

can't = can not = cannot

6 GRAMMAR PRACTICE Complete each conversation with <u>can</u> or <u>can't</u> and the base form of a verb.

1 A: .... you .... the guitar?

B: Yes, I .... But I don't play well.

2 A: .... Gwen .... well?

B: Yes, she .... She swims very well.

3 A: .... your brother ....?

B: My brother? No. He .... cook at all.

4 A: .... Gloria .... English well?

B: No, she .... She needs this class.

5 A: .... your mother ....?

B: Yes. She knits very well.

6 A: .... your sisters ....?

B: Yes. They go skiing every weekend.

NOW YOU CAN Express a wish

1 5:04 🔊 **CONVERSATION MODEL** Read and listen.

A: I wish I could draw. Can you?

B: Yes, I can.

A: Really?

B: I draw a lot. But not very well.

2 5:05 🔊 **RHYTHM AND INTONATION** Listen again and repeat. Then practice the Conversation Model with a partner.

3 **PAIR WORK** Personalize the conversation. Express a wish and ask about your partner's abilities. Then change roles.

A: I wish I could .... Can you?

B: ....

A: Really?

B: ....

Don't stop!
Ask more questions. Say more about your abilities.

♻ **Be sure to recycle this language.**

What do you [draw]?   I draw [people].
When do you [ski]?   I ski [every weekend].
Where do you [sing]?   I sing [in the shower].

4 **CHANGE PARTNERS** Express other wishes.

GOAL   Politely decline an invitation

5:06

1 🔊 **VOCABULARY** • *Reasons for not doing something* Read and listen. Then listen again and repeat.

1 She's busy.

2 They're not hungry.

3 She's full.

4 He's tired.

5 It's early.

6 It's late.

2 **PAIR WORK** Tell your partner about a time you were busy, tired, or full.

> ❝ Last week, I worked late every day. I was so tired. ❞

3 **GRAMMAR** • *Too + adjective*

Too makes an adjective stronger. It usually gives it a negative meaning.
I'm **too busy**. I can't talk right now.
I'm **too tired**. Let's not go to the movies.
It's **too late**. I should go to bed.

Be careful!
Don't use <u>too</u> with a positive adjective.
　She's so pretty.
　NOT She's ~~too pretty~~.

4 **GRAMMAR PRACTICE** Complete each sentence. Use <u>too</u> and an adjective.

1 I don't want these shoes.
They're *too expensive* .

2 It's .... today.
She can't go swimming.

3 I'm ....
I can't read right now.

4 He doesn't want that shirt.
It's ....

5 I can't talk right now.
I'm ....

6 It's ....
I don't want to watch a movie.

Politely decline an invitation

1 🔊 **CONVERSATION MODEL** Read and listen.
5:07

A: Let's go to a movie.

B: I'm really sorry, but I'm too busy.

A: That's too bad. Maybe some other time.

2 🔊 **RHYTHM AND INTONATION** Listen again
5:08
and repeat. Then practice the Conversation
Model with a partner.

3 **PAIR WORK** Change the model. Suggest a
different activity. Use the vocabulary and the
photos (or your own ideas). Then change roles.

A: Let's go ....

B: I'm really sorry, but ....

A: .... Maybe some other time.

> **Don't stop!**
> Suggest another activity.
> Accept or decline the invitation.

♻ **Be sure to recycle this language.**

How about ___ ?	[go] for a drive
Sounds great.	[go] bike riding
OK.	[go] for a walk

to a game

to a restaurant

to the park

to a concert

to the beach

4 **CHANGE PARTNERS** Suggest other activities and give other reasons.

GOAL   Ask for and agree to do a favor

1 GRAMMAR *Polite requests with* <u>Could you</u> + *base form*

> Use <u>Could you</u> and the base form of a verb to make requests.
>   **Could you wash** the dishes?
> Use <u>please</u> to make a request more polite.
>   Could you **please** wash the dishes?

5:09

2 ◀))) **VOCABULARY** • *Favors* Read and listen. Then listen again and repeat.

1 Could you please **open** the window?

Also: open the door
open the refrigerator

2 Could you please **close** the door?

Also: close the window
close the microwave door

3 Could you please **turn on** the light?

Also: turn on the stove
turn on the computer

4 Could you please **turn off** the TV?

Also: turn off the microwave
turn off the light

5 Could you please **hand me** my glasses?

Also: hand me my sweater
hand me my book

6 Could you please **help me**?

Also: give me a hand

3 INTEGRATED PRACTICE Complete the polite requests. Use <u>Could you please</u>. Use the Vocabulary and other verbs you know.

1 It's a little hot in here. .... the window?

2 I have a headache. .... dinner tonight?

3 I'm going shopping. .... my jacket?

4 I'm going to bed. .... the computer?

5 I want to read a book. .... the lamp?

6 .... shopping? We need milk.

7 I'm making dinner right now. .... out the garbage?

8 Let's watch a movie. .... the TV?

4 🔊 **LISTENING COMPREHENSION** Listen to the conversations. Then complete each request.

5:10

1 Could you *close the window* ...., please?

2 Could you ....?

3 Could you please ....?

4 Could you please ....?

5 Could you ....?

5:11

5 🔊 **PRONUNCIATION** • *Assimilation of sounds: Could you...?* Read and listen. Then listen again and repeat.

/ˈkʊdʒu/   /ˈkʊdʒu/

1 Could you please open the window?   **2** Could you please close the door?

6 **INTEGRATED PRACTICE** Look again at the Vocabulary. Choose three requests to read aloud. Pay attention to assimilation of sounds in Could you.

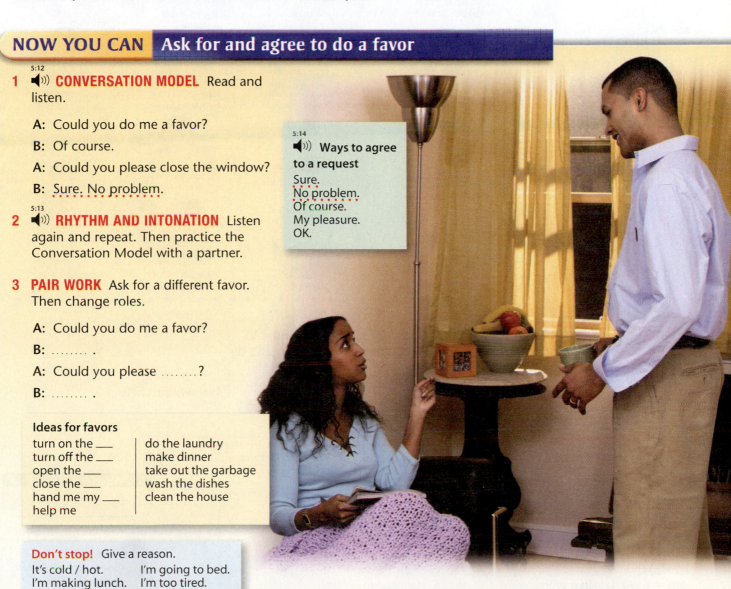

NOW YOU CAN Ask for and agree to do a favor

5:12

1 🔊 **CONVERSATION MODEL** Read and listen.

A: Could you do me a favor?

B: Of course.

A: Could you please close the window?

B: Sure. No problem.

5:14

🔊 **Ways to agree to a request**
Sure.
No problem.
Of course.
My pleasure.
OK.

5:13

2 🔊 **RHYTHM AND INTONATION** Listen again and repeat. Then practice the Conversation Model with a partner.

3 **PAIR WORK** Ask for a different favor. Then change roles.

A: Could you do me a favor?

B: ....

A: Could you please ....?

B: ....

Ideas for favors

turn on the ___	do the laundry
turn off the ___	make dinner
open the ___	take out the garbage
close the ___	wash the dishes
hand me my ___	clean the house
help me	

Don't stop! Give a reason.
It's cold / hot.   I'm going to bed.
I'm making lunch.   I'm too tired.

4 **CHANGE PARTNERS** Ask for other favors.

More Practice
ActiveBook Self-Study Disc

grammar · vocabulary · listening
reading · speaking · pronunciation

1 🔊 5:15 **READING** Read the article.

From infant to toddler...

At birth, an infant cannot do anything alone.
But before the age of two, a baby learns many things.

lie   sit   crawl   walk

Between 1 and 3 months a baby can...
- turn her head or smile when her mother or father speaks.
- roll over.
- cry when she's hungry, thirsty, or afraid.
- see colors.

Between 3 and 6 months a baby can...
- sit with help.
- reach for things.
- look at his own hands and feet.
- laugh and make an "m" sound.

Between 6 and 12 months a baby can...
- crawl and stand.
- sit without help and pick up small things.
- say some words.

Between 1 and 2 years a baby can...
- throw things.
- say "no".
- play next to other children.
- walk.

2 READING COMPREHENSION Write ✓ for the things that five-month-old
babies can do, according to the article. Write ✗ for the things they can't do.

- ☐ smile
- ☐ pick up small things
- ☐ see colors
- ☐ say some words
- ☐ walk
- ☐ roll over
- ☐ crawl and stand
- ☐ reach for things
- ☐ laugh
- ☐ throw things
- ☐ sit without help

3 INTEGRATED PRACTICE Complete the sentences
about what a baby <u>cannot</u> do.

On your *ActiveBook* Self-Study Disc:
Extra Reading Comprehension Questions

> At one month, *a baby can't crawl.*

1 At two months,
2 At five months,
3 At eleven months,
4 At sixteen months,

GRAMMAR BOOSTER
Extra practice • p.145

🎵 5:16/5:17
Top Notch Pop
"She Can't Play Guitar"
Lyrics p. 148

4 GROUP WORK Discuss things children can and
can't do at other ages.

❝ At three years, a child can't ride a bicycle. ❞   ❝ At eight years, a child can do some household chores. ❞

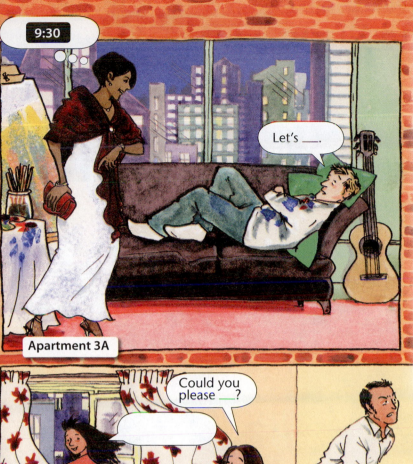

Apartment 3A

PAIR WORK

1 Create conversations for the people.

A: Let's ___ .
B: What time is it?

2 Ask and answer questions with <u>Can</u> about the people. For example:

Can she ___ ? / Can he ___ ?

GAME Make a false statement about the picture, using <u>too</u> and an adjective. Your partner explains why it's false. For example:

A: Apartment 2A is too warm.
B: False, because the woman is cold.

STORY Create a story about what is happening in the apartment building. Start like this:

It's 9:30...

WRITING Describe some things people can and can't do when they get old. For example:

At eighty, some people can't drive, but my grandfather can.

Apartment 2A

Apartment 2B

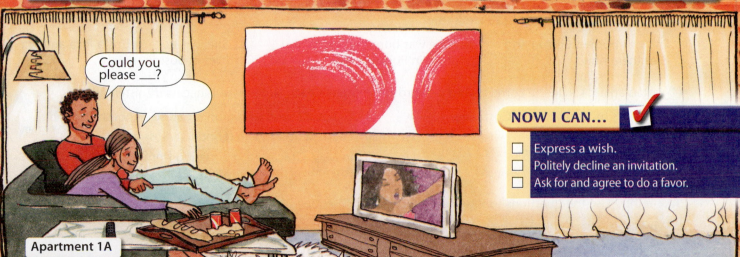

Apartment 1A

NOW I CAN... ✓

☐ Express a wish.
☐ Politely decline an invitation.
☐ Ask for and agree to do a favor.

Life Events and Plans

GOALS After Unit 14, you will be able to:

1 Get to know someone's life story.
2 Discuss plans.
3 Express wishes for the future.

LESSON 1

GOAL Get to know someone's life story

1 ◀)) **VOCABULARY** • *Some life events* Read and listen. Then listen again and repeat.
5:18

1 be born

2 grow up

3 go to school

4 move

5 study

6 graduate

2 ◀)) **PRONUNCIATION** • *Diphthongs* Listen and repeat.
5:19

1 /aɪ/	2 /aʊ/	3 /ɔɪ/
my	how	boy
I	noun	oil
tie	town	boil

3 **PRONUNCIATION PRACTICE** Look at the Vocabulary pictures. Ask and answer the questions out loud with a partner. Use the correct pronunciation of the diphthongs.

1 What's the boy's first name?
2 What's his last name?
3 What school did he go to?
4 What university did he graduate from?

4 ◀)) **LISTENING COMPREHENSION** Listen to the conversation about Graciela Boyd's life story. Which statement about Graciela's life is true?
5:20

☐ She was born in Boston and lives there now.

☐ She was born in London and lives in Boston now.

☐ She was born in Costa Rica and lives in Boston now.

◀)) Listen again. Circle the correct word or words to complete each statement. If necessary, listen again.

1 Graciela's mother is from (Costa Rica / Boston).

2 Graciela was born in (Costa Rica / London).

3 Her father is (American / British).

4 Graciela's mother is a/an (Spanish / English) teacher.

5 Graciela grew up in (London / Boston).

6 In May, Graciela is graduating from (the university / medical school).

5 **PAIR WORK** Use the questions to interview your partner. Then tell the class about your partner.

1 When and where were you born? What about other people in your family?

2 Where did you grow up? What about other people in your family?

5:21

6 ◀)) **VOCABULARY** • *Academic subjects* Read and listen.
Then listen again and repeat.

1 architecture

2 medicine

3 psychology

4 business

5 education

6 mathematics / math

7 information technology

8 nursing

9 engineering

10 law

NOW YOU CAN Get to know someone's life story

5:22

1 ◀)) **CONVERSATION MODEL** Read and listen.

A: Where were you born?

B: Here. In New York.

A: And did you grow up here?

B: Yes, I did. And you?

A: I was born in Brasilia.

B: Did you grow up there?

A: Actually, no. I grew up in Toronto.

5:23

2 ◀)) **RHYTHM AND INTONATION** Listen again and repeat. Then practice the Conversation Model with a partner.

3 **PAIR WORK** Personalize the conversation with real information.

A: Where were you born?

B: ....

A: And did you grow up ....?

B: .... And you?

A: I was born in ....

B: Did you grow up ....?

A: ....

Don't stop! Ask and answer more questions.

♻ **Be sure to recycle this language.**

What do you do?
What are you studying
[or What did you study]?
Did you graduate?

4 **CHANGE PARTNERS** Get to know another classmate's life story.

GOAL   Discuss plans

VOCABULARY BOOSTER
More leisure activities • p. 135

1 🔊 5:24 **VOCABULARY** • *More leisure activities* Read and listen. Then listen again and repeat.

1 travel   **2** go camping   **3** go fishing   **4** relax

5 hang out with friends   **6** sleep late   **7** do nothing

Also remember
check e-mail
exercise
go dancing
go out for dinner
go running
go to the beach
go to the movies
listen to music
paint
play soccer
read
take a nap
visit friends

2 🔊 5:25 **LISTENING COMPREHENSION** Listen to the cell phone calls. Complete each sentence with the present continuous form of one of the words or phrases in the Vocabulary.

1 Charlie's   *doing nothing* ....

2 Rachel's ....

3 They're ....

4 Barbara's ....

5 Harvey's family is ....

3 GRAMMAR • *Be going to + base form*

> **Use <u>be going to</u> + base form to express future plans.**
>
> I'm
> You're
> He's
> She's   } **going to relax** this weekend.
> We're
> They're
>
> I'm
> You're
> He's
> She's   } **not going to go** camping this weekend.
> We're
> They're
>
> **Contractions**
> is not going = **'s not going** = **isn't going**
> are not going = **'re not going** = **aren't going**
>
> <u>Yes</u> / <u>no</u> questions
> **Are** you **going to sleep** late tomorrow?   Yes, I am. / No, I'm not.
> **Is** she **going to travel** to Europe?   Yes, she is. / No, she isn't.
> **Are** we **going to be** on time?   Yes, we are. / No, we aren't.

4 GRAMMAR PRACTICE Write sentences about future plans with <u>be going to</u>.

1 you / eat in a restaurant / this weekend? *Are you going to eat in a restaurant this weekend?*

2 They / go to the movies / tonight. ....

3 I / hang out with my parents / at the beach. ....

4 he / relax / tomorrow? ....

5 she / go fishing / with you? ....

6 we / exercise / on Saturday? ....

7 they / move? ....

8 Jeff and Joan / study / architecture. ....

9 She / graduate / in May. ....

NOW YOU CAN Discuss plans

1 🔊 5:26 **CONVERSATION MODEL** Read and listen.

A: Any plans for the weekend?

B: Not really. I'm just going to hang out with friends. And you?

A: Actually, I'm going to go camping.

2 🔊 5:27 **RHYTHM AND INTONATION** Listen again and repeat. Then practice the Conversation Model with a partner.

3 **PAIR WORK** Personalize the conversation. Use the Vocabulary or the pictures below and <u>be going to</u>.

A: Any plans for ....?

B: .... I'm .... And you?

A: Actually, I'm ....

Don't stop!
Ask about other times. Ask more questions with <u>be going to</u>.

 Be sure to recycle this language.

next week
after class
Are you going to ___ ?

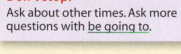

4 **CHANGE PARTNERS** Ask another classmate about his or her plans.

115

GOAL	**Express wishes for the future**

1 🔊 **VOCABULARY** • *Life cycle events* Read and listen. Then listen again and repeat.

5:28

1 get married

2 have children

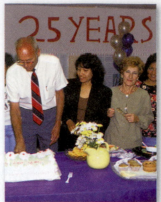
3 retire

4 change careers

2 GRAMMAR • *Would like + infinitive: statements and yes/no questions*

We'd like to get married.

Use would like + an infinitive to express your wishes for the future.

infinitive

She**'d like**   **to study** art.
They **wouldn't like**   **to have** children.

Contractions
would like → 'd like
would not like → wouldn't like

Yes / no questions

Would you **like to change** careers?   Yes, I would. / No, I wouldn't.
Would they **like to get** married?   Yes, they would. / No, they wouldn't.

3 🔊 **LISTENING COMPREHENSION** Listen to each person. Then complete each sentence with <u>would like</u>. Use the infinitive form of a word or phrase from the Vocabulary.

5:29

1 She *would like to get married* .   **3** She ....

2 He ....   **4** They ....

4 INTEGRATED PRACTICE Complete the survey. Then, on a separate sheet of paper, write statements about yourself, using <u>would like</u> and <u>wouldn't like</u> + infinitives.

In the next two years, would you like to...

- ☐ get married?
- ☐ graduate?
- ☐ have children?
- ☐ move to a new country?
- ☐ move to a new city?
- ☐ move to a new apartment or a new house?

- ☐ study a new language?
- ☐ write a book?
- ☐ learn to play a musical instrument?
- ☐ get a new car?
- ☐ meet a good-looking man?
- ☐ meet a good-looking woman?

- ☐ meet a Scorpio?
- ☐ paint your living room?
- ☐ buy a new refrigerator?
- ☐ OTHER   *I'd like to...*
  _____
  _____

5 PAIR WORK Ask your partner questions from the survey in Exercise 4. Would you both like to do the same things? Or would you like to do different things?

6 GRAMMAR *Would like + infinitive: information questions*

> **What would** you **like** to study? (Business.)
> **When would** they **like** to retire? (In June.)
> **Where would** he **like** to go next weekend? (To the movies.)
> **Who would** you **like** to marry? (Elena.)
>
> **BUT: Note the difference in word order when <u>Who</u> is the subject:**
> **Who would like** to study Italian? (I would!)

7 INTEGRATED PRACTICE Write information questions with <u>would like</u>, using the cues.

1 Where / you / get married *Where would you like to get married?* ....

2 What / their children / study ....

3 What / her husband / do ....

4 When / your parents / move ....

5 Who / her daughter / marry ....

6 Who / change careers ....

NOW YOU CAN Express wishes for the future

1 **CONVERSATION MODEL** Read and listen.

A: So what's next for you, Shawn?

B: What do you mean?

A: Well, would you like to get married or have children?

B: Actually, yes. I'd like to get married <u>and</u> have children. What about you?

A: Me? Actually, I'd like to study art.

2 **RHYTHM AND INTONATION** Listen again and repeat. Then practice the Conversation Model with a partner.

3 PAIR WORK Personalize the conversation. Use the Vocabulary from page 116 and real information.

A: So what's next for you, ...?

B: What do you mean?

A: Well, would you like to ....?

B: Actually, ... I'd like to .... What about you?

A: Me? Actually, I'd like to ....

Don't stop!
Continue asking about other wishes for the future.
• graduate
• study [nursing]
• move to ___
• get a new job
• meet my future [husband / wife]

4 CHANGE PARTNERS Ask another classmate what he or she would like to do.

1 〔5:32 〕 🔊 **READING** Read about Harry Houdini, a famous escape artist.

The Amazing Houdini

Harry Houdini was born Ehrich Weisz in Budapest, Hungary, on March 24, 1874. He came from a large family. He had six siblings—five brothers and one sister.

At the age of four, Ehrich moved with his family to the United States, first to Appleton, Wisconsin, and then later to New York City.

The family was poor, and young Ehrich didn't get an education and never graduated from school. Instead, he worked to help the family. Ehrich and his brother Theo were interested in magic, and at the age of seventeen, Ehrich began his career as a magician. He changed his name to Houdini, after the name of a famous French magician, Robert Houdin.

In 1893, Houdini married Beatrice Raymond, whom he called Bess. For the rest of Houdini's career, Bess worked as his assistant on stage. The couple didn't have children.

At first, Houdini wasn't very successful. But in 1899, he started to do "escape acts," in which he escaped from chains and handcuffs. People came to see him escape from chains and boxes underwater. In one famous act, Houdini escaped from a large milk can filled with milk. Houdini became rich and famous all over the world.

In 1926, Houdini was sick during a performance. After the show, he went to the hospital. But it was too late—Harry Houdini died at the young age of 52.

HOUDINI'S DEATH-DEFYING MYSTERY
ESCAPE FROM A GALVANIZED IRON CAN FILLED WITH WATER AND SECURED BY MASSIVE LOCKS

FAILURE MEANS A DROWNING DEATH

Information source: http://www.apl.org

On your *ActiveBook* Self-Study Disc:
Extra Reading Comprehension Questions

2 READING COMPREHENSION Answer the questions in complete sentences.

1 What was Houdini's original name? ....

2 Where was he born? ....

3 When did his family move? ....

4 Where did they move? ....

5 Did Houdini graduate from a university? ....

6 Did Houdini get married? ....

7 What was his wife's name? ....

8 Did the Houdinis have children? ....

9 When did Houdini die? ....

10 **Challenge:** What would you like to know more about? On a separate sheet of paper, write three information questions. Example:

> *Why did Houdini's family move to the United States?*

GRAMMAR BOOSTER

Extra practice • p. 146

〔5:33/5:34〕
🎵 **Top Notch Pop**
"I Wasn't Born Yesterday"
Lyrics p. 148

3 PAIR WORK Tell your partner your life story. Ask your partner questions about his or her story.

Lauren Denmark
Born May 12, 1990
New York (U.S.)

PAIR WORK Ask and answer questions about Lauren's life. Ask about her plans and her wishes for the future.
For example:

Where was Lauren born?

TELL A STORY Tell the story of Lauren Denmark's life. Talk about the past, the present, and the future. What did she do? What is she doing now? What would she like to do? Start like this:

Lauren was born in 1990. She grew up in ...

WRITING On a separate sheet of paper, write the story of your own life. Then write your plans and wishes for the future. Include a picture or pictures if possible.
For example:

I was born in Madrid in 1987. I grew up in ...

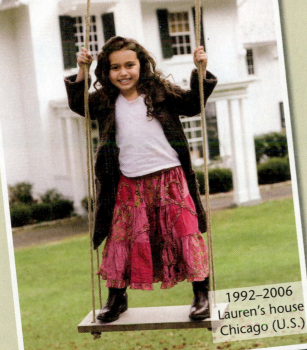

1992–2006
Lauren's house
Chicago (U.S.)

May 21, 2010
Barton College of Engineering Los Angeles (U.S.)

Next year she'd like...

In three years she'd like...

Today
San Francisco (U.S.)

NOW I CAN... ✔

- [ ] Get to know someone's life story.
- [ ] Discuss plans.
- [ ] Express wishes for the future.

1 🔊 **LISTENING COMPREHENSION** Listen to the conversations. Check the picture that answers each question.

1 Where does he live?

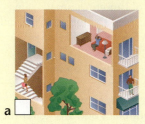 a ☐    b ☐

2 Where does he work?

 a ☐    b ☐

3 Where does she work?

 a ☐    b ☐

4 Where does she teach?

 a ☐    b ☐

5 Where does she work?

 a ☐   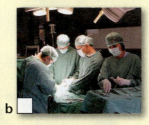 b ☐

6 Where does his daughter work?

 a ☐    b ☐

2 **INTEGRATED PRACTICE** Complete the e-mail about Anna's new apartment. Use <u>there's</u> and <u>there are</u>, and the names of furniture and appliances.

My new apartment!

Hey, Mel: I have this great furnished apartment. It has everything! The .... 1 .... has a nice big stove and four .... 2 .... There's a dining room with a .... 3 .... and four .... 4 .... Next to the dining room .... 5 .... a large living room with a green .... 6 .... And .... 7 .... four chairs: great for hanging out with my friends and watching .... 8 .... There's no office, but there's a .... 9 .... in the living room. And I love the bedroom. It has a .... 10 .... for all my books. There are two .... 11 .... and two blue .... 12 .... Very nice! There's even a beautiful balcony next to the bedroom, with a little .... 13 .... and two .... 14 .... The bathroom is the only room that isn't perfect. .... 15 .... a shower but no .... 16 ....

3 GRAMMAR PRACTICE Write questions about home and work. Use <u>What</u>, <u>Where</u>, <u>Is there</u>, and <u>Are there</u>. Ask your partner the questions. Write your partner's answers.

	Your questions		Your answers
1		1	
2		2	
3		3	
4		4	
5		5	
6		6	

4 GRAMMAR PRACTICE Complete the conversations with the correct forms of the verbs.

1 A: Where .... Jill .... last weekend?
          go

   B: I'm not sure. I know she .... to
                   want
     go camping.

   A: Maybe she .... camping, then.
                go

2 A: Would you like to go to the beach?

   B: No way. We .... there yesterday.
               be

     We .... an awful time.
         have

   A: Why? What .... wrong?
            be

   B: The water .... really dirty,
          be

     so I .... swimming.
       not go

3 A: Where .... you this morning?
             be

   B: Me? I .... running.
           go

   A: Did Sheri .... with you?
           go

   B: No. She .... to class.
           go

4 A: .... you .... yesterday?
                 work

   B: No, I .... Yesterday I .... sick.
                      be

   A: I'm sorry. .... you .... a fever?
                   have

   B: Yes, I ....

5 CONVERSATION PRACTICE
Use the questions you wrote in Grammar Practice 3. Exchange real information about where you live and work. Start like this:

> "What's your apartment like?"

Ideas
- the location of your home, school, and workplace
- the places in your neighborhood
- the description of your home

6 GRAMMAR PRACTICE Complete the telephone conversations with the present continuous or the simple present tense.

1 A: Hello?

B: Hi, Sid. Ann. .... ?

you /sleep

A: No, I'm not. .... breakfast.

I / make

B: .... breakfast?

you / usually / make

A: Actually, ... often.

I / not cook

But .... for a test.

Gwen / study

2 A: Hello?

B: Hi, Bonnie. .... for food.

I / shop

.... anything from the store?

you / need

A: Actually yes. .... a salad for

I / make

dinner and .... any tomatoes.

I / not have

B: No problem. .... those

They / sell

beautiful tomatoes from Mexico right now.

A: Great! .... those tomatoes.

I / like

3 A: Hello?

B: Hi, Liz. Where are you?

A: .... right now. Can I

I / drive

call you back?

B: Sure. .... my office

you have

number? .... today.

I / work

4 A: Hello?

B: Hi, Stan. What time ....

you / get up

on Saturdays?

A: Why .... that now?

you / ask

It's only Thursday!

B: Because .... her driving

Maria / take

test at 8:30, and .... a ride to

she / need

the test.

7 PAIR WORK Partner A: Look at your picture.
Partner B: Turn your book and look at your picture.
Ask questions about the foods on the table.

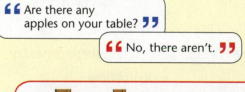
Are there any apples on your table?
No, there aren't.

PARTNER A

PARTNER B

8 INTEGRATED PRACTICE Write questions to complete each conversation.

1 A: ....?

B: I usually eat lunch at the office.

2 A: ....?

B: Dana and Eric? They went to Colorado.

3 A: ....?

B: Milk? We need two large containers.

4 A: ....?

B: Sally teaches math.

5 A: ....?

B: Madhur was born in India.

6 A: ....?

B: I'd like to study architecture.

7 A: ....?

B: No. I'm not going to graduate this year.

8 A: ....?

B: She broke her leg.

9 A: ....?

B: Oh, that's Juliette Binoche, the actress.

10 A: ....?

B: Yes, my parents can speak Arabic, but I can't.

9 🔊 **LISTENING COMPREHENSION** Listen to the conversations. Check past, present, or future. Then listen again and check your work.

	Past	Present	Future
1	☐	☑	☐
2	☐	☐	☐
3	☐	☐	☐
4	☐	☐	☐
5	☐	☐	☐
6	☐	☐	☐

10 INTEGRATED PRACTICE Express sympathy to each person. Make suggestions with <u>should</u> and <u>shouldn't</u>.

1
I have a terrible headache.

YOU *I'm so sorry* . You *should take something* .
....

2
My husband burned his mouth with the soup.

YOU .... He
....
....

3
My brother and I have stomachaches. I think we ate something bad.

YOU .... You
....
....

4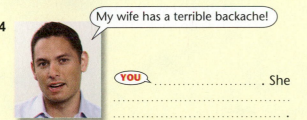
My wife has a terrible backache!

YOU .... She
....
....

5
I didn't sleep last night. I feel terrible!

YOU .... You
....
....

6
My son has an earache and a fever. He's only eighteen months old.

YOU .... He
....
....

7
My grandfather fell down and broke his arm when the weather was bad.

YOU .... He
....
....

11 CONVERSATION PRACTICE Discuss relatives and friends. Start like this:

Ideas
- Appearance
- Studies
- Abilities
- Life events
- Wishes for the future

❝ Tell me about your mother. Where was she born? ❞

♻ **Be sure to recycle this language.**

Tell me about ___ .
Really?
No kidding.

Reference Charts

Countries and nationalities

Country	Nationality	Country	Nationality	Country	Nationality
Argentina	Argentinean / Argentine	Guatemala	Guatemalan	Peru	Peruvian
Australia	Australian	Holland	Dutch	Poland	Polish
Belgium	Belgian	Honduras	Honduran	Portugal	Portuguese
Bolivia	Bolivian	Hungary	Hungarian	Russia	Russian
Brazil	Brazilian	India	Indian	Saudi Arabia	Saudi / Saudi Arabian
Canada	Canadian	Indonesia	Indonesian	Spain	Spanish
Chile	Chilean	Ireland	Irish	Sweden	Swedish
China	Chinese	Italy	Italian	Switzerland	Swiss
Colombia	Colombian	Japan	Japanese	Taiwan	Chinese
Costa Rica	Costa Rican	Korea	Korean	Thailand	Thai
Ecuador	Ecuadorian	Lebanon	Lebanese	Turkey	Turkish
Egypt	Egyptian	Malaysia	Malaysian	the United Kingdom	British
El Salvador	Salvadorean	Mexico	Mexican	the United States	American
France	French	Nicaragua	Nicaraguan	Uruguay	Uruguayan
Germany	German	Panama	Panamanian	Venezuela	Venezuelan
Greece	Greek	Paraguay	Paraguayan	Vietnam	Vietnamese

Numbers 100 to 1,000,000,000

100	one hundred	1,000	one thousand	10,000	ten thousand	1,000,000	one million
500	five hundred	5,000	five thousand	100,000	one hundred thousand	1,000,000,000	one billion

Irregular verbs

This is an alphabetical list of all irregular verbs in the *Top Notch Fundamentals* units. The page number refers to the page on which the base form of the verb first appears.

base form	simple past	page	base form	simple past	page	base form	simple past	page
be	was / were	4	get	got	52	say	said	90
break	broke	98	go	went	25	see	saw	85
buy	bought	76	grow	grew	112	sing	sang	104
can	could	23	hang out	hung out	114	sleep	slept	114
come	came	52	have	had	32	study	studied	52
cut	cut	98	hurt	hurt	98	swim	swam	104
do	did	52	lie	lay	100	take	took	22
draw	drew	104	make	made	52	teach	taught	84
drink	drank	85	meet	met	1	tell	told	88
drive	drove	22	put	put	52	think	thought	90
eat	ate	52	read	read	54	wear	wore	72
fall	fell	98	ride	rode	92	write	wrote	5
feel	felt	100						

Pronunciation table

These are the pronunciation symbols used in *Top Notch Fundamentals*.

Vowels

Symbol	Key Words	Symbol	Key Words
i	feed	ə	banana, around
ɪ	did	ɚ	shirt, birthday
eɪ	date, table	aɪ	cry, eye
ɛ	bed, neck	aʊ	about, how
æ	bad, hand	ɔɪ	boy
ɑ	box, father	ɪr	here, near
ɔ	wash	ɛr	chair
oʊ	comb, post	ɑr	guitar, are
ʊ	book, good	ɔr	door, chore
u	boot, food, student	ʊr	tour
ʌ	but, mother		

Consonants

Symbol	Key Words	Symbol	Key Words
p	park, happy	t̬	butter, bottle
b	back, cabbage	t˺	button
t	tie	ʃ	she, station, special, discussion
d	die		
k	came, kitchen, quarter	ʒ	leisure
g	game, go	h	hot, who
tʃ	chicken, watch	m	men
dʒ	jacket, orange	n	sun, know
f	face, photographer	ŋ	sung, singer
v	vacation	w	week, white
θ	thing, math	l	light, long
ð	then, that	r	rain, writer
s	city, psychology	y	yes, use, music
z	please, goes		

Vocabulary Booster

5:37
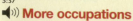 **More occupations**

1 an accountant

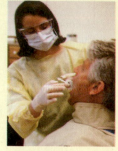

2 a bank teller

3 a dentist

4 an electrician

5 a florist

6 a gardener

7 a grocery clerk

8 a hairdresser

9 a mechanic

10 a pharmacist

11 a professor

12 a reporter

13 a salesperson

14 a travel agent

15 a secretary

16 a waiter

17 a nurse

18 a lawyer

On a separate sheet of paper, write five statements about the pictures. Use <u>He</u> or <u>She</u> and the verb <u>be</u>. For example: *He's an accountant.*

5:38
 More relationships

5:39
 More titles

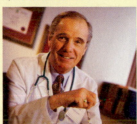

1 a supervisor
2 an employee

3 a teammate

1 Doctor [Smith] or Dr. [Smith]

2 Professor [Brown]

3 Captain [Jones]

On a separate sheet of paper, write three statements about the photos, using <u>He's</u> or <u>She's</u> and possessive adjectives. For example: *She's her supervisor.*

UNIT 3

5:40
 More places in the neighborhood

1 a clothing store

2 an electronics store

3 a fire station

4 a police station

5 a shoe store

6 a toy store

7 a video store

8 a dry cleaners

9 a gas station

10 a hotel

11 a supermarket

12 a convenience store

13 a travel agency

14 a post office

15 a taxi stand

On a separate sheet of paper, write five questions about the places. For example:

Where's the clothing store?
Can I walk to the hotel?

5:41

🔊 **More adjectives to describe people**

1 slim / thin

2 muscular

3 heavy

On a separate sheet of paper, write a sentence for each photo. Use a form of <u>be</u> and the adverb <u>very</u> or <u>so</u>. For example: *He's very ___.*

UNIT 5

5:42

🔊 **More events**

1 an exhibition

2 an opera

3 a ballet

4 a football game

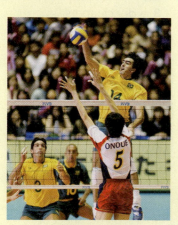

5 a volleyball game

6 a baseball game

7 a play

8 a speech

On a separate sheet of paper, write five statements about the events. Use your own times and dates.
For example: *There's an exhibition on Tuesday, June 15.*

5:43
🔊 **More clothes**

1 bathing suits / swimsuits

2 a bathrobe

3 boots

4 a coat

5 a hat

6 a shirt
7 jeans

8 a nightgown

9 an umbrella
10 a raincoat

11 sandals

12 pajamas

13 a T-shirt
14 shorts

15 socks

16 pantyhose

17 underwear

On a separate sheet of paper, write five questions and answers about the colors of the clothes and shoes. For example:

What color are the boots? They're brown.

5:44
🔊 **More household chores**

1 dust

2 sweep

3 mop

4 vacuum

Who does these chores in your house? On a separate sheet of paper, write four statements, using the simple present tense and frequency adverbs or time expressions.
For example: *I usually dust once a week.*

5:45

🔊 **More home and office vocabulary**

4 an intercom **5** a doorbell

1 a fence **2** a driveway **3** a roof

7 a pillow

8 a blanket
9 a sheet

6 a fire escape

10 a medicine cabinet   **13** a shower curtain
11 toothpaste   **14** a bath mat
12 a toothbrush

15 towels

16 a faucet

17 a burner
18 an oven

19 a dishwasher

20 a coffee maker

21 a ladle
22 a pot

23 a food processor

24 a napkin
25 a place mat
26 a glass

27 a bowl   **29** a cup
28 a plate **30** a saucer

31 a fork
32 a knife
33 a tablespoon /
    a soup spoon
34 a teaspoon

On a separate sheet of paper, write five statements.
Use the Vocabulary. For example:

My apartment has a fire escape.
There's no shower curtain in my bathroom.

35 a filing cabinet

36 a fax machine

5:46
◀)) **More weather vocabulary**

1 a thunderstorm

2 a snowstorm

3 a hurricane

4 a tornado

5:47
◀)) **Seasons**

1 spring

2 summer

3 fall / autumn

4 winter

On a separate sheet of paper, write four statements about the pictures.
For example: *It's not raining.*

5:48

🔊 **More vegetables**

1 carrots
2 cabbage
3 broccoli
4 cauliflower
5 leeks
6 cucumbers
7 brussels sprouts

8 corn

9 lettuce
10 asparagus
11 an eggplant
12 beans
13 peas
14 celery

15 garlic

5:49

🔊 **More fruits**

1 a tangerine
2 a grapefruit
3 a lemon
4 a lime
5 an orange

9 a pear

10 apricots

11 peaches

6 grapes
7 a pineapple
8 bananas

12 strawberries

13 raspberries

19 a watermelon

14 a honeydew melon
15 an avocado
16 a papaya
17 a mango
18 a kiwi

20 raisins
21 figs
22 prunes
23 dates

On a separate sheet of paper, write five statements about the fruits and vegetables you and your family like.
For example: *I like lemons. My sister doesn't like lemons.*

5:50
🔊 **More outdoor activities**

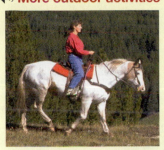

1 go horseback riding

2 go sailing

3 play golf

4 go rollerblading

5 go snorkeling

On a separate sheet of paper, write
five sentences to describe the photos.
Use the simple past tense.
For example: *They went sailing.*

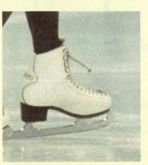

6 go rock climbing

7 go ice skating

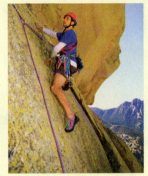

8 go windsurfing

5:51
🔊 **More parts of the body**

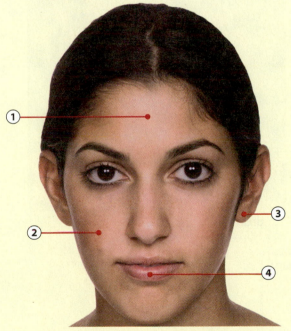

5 tongue

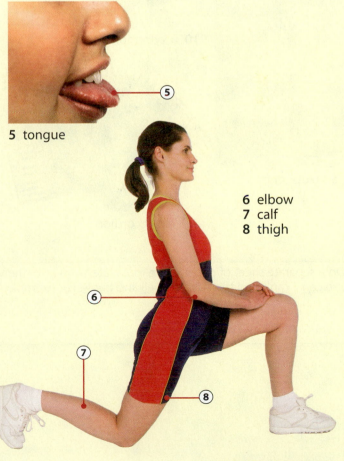

1 forehead   **3** earlobe
2 cheek   **4** lip

6 elbow
7 calf
8 thigh

On a separate sheet of paper, describe
one of the people. Write three statements.
Use the Vocabulary from Unit 12.
For example: *She has straight, brown hair.*

Vocabulary Booster   **133**

5:52

◀))) More musical instruments

1 a cello

2 a piano

3 a tuba

4 a trumpet

5 a trombone

6 a flute

7 a clarinet

8 a recorder

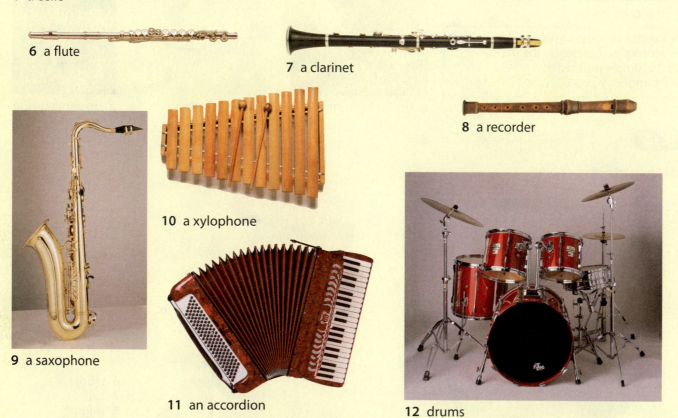

9 a saxophone

10 a xylophone

11 an accordion

12 drums

On a separate sheet of paper, write four statements with the Vocabulary.
Use <u>can</u> / <u>can't</u> and the adverbs <u>well</u> and <u>badly</u>. For example:

My sister can play the piano.
My father plays the accordion well.

5:53

🔊 **More academic subjects**

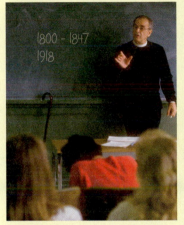

1 biology

2 chemistry

3 history

4 fine art

5 drama

6 science

5:54

🔊 **More leisure activities**

1 go skiing

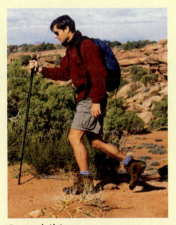

2 go hiking

3 play

4 garden

5 go on a cruise

6 get a manicure

On a separate sheet of paper, write four statements, using I'd like to or be going to and the Vocabulary. Include time expressions. For example:

I'd like to study fine art in the future.

I'm not going to go on a cruise this year.

Grammar Booster

The Grammar Booster is optional. It contains extra practice of each unit's grammar.

1 Write each sentence again. Use a contraction.

1 He is an engineer. _He's an engineer._

2 We are teachers. _____

3 No, we are not. _____

4 They are not artists. _____

5 I am a student. _____

6 She is a chef. _____

2 Write the indefinite article _a_ or _an_ for each occupation.

1 _____ chef

2 _____ actor

3 _____ banker

4 _____ musician

5 _____ scientist

6 _____ architect

7 _____ photographer

3 Complete each sentence with the correct subject pronoun.

1 Mary is a student. _She_ is a student.

2 Ben is a student, too. _____ is a student, too.

3 My name is Nora. _____ am an artist.

4 Your occupation is doctor. _____ are a doctor.

5 Jane and Jason are scientists. _____ are scientists.

4 Write a question for each answer.

1 A: _Are you musicians_ ?
   B: Yes, we are. We're musicians.

2 A: _____ ?
   B: No, they're not teachers. They're scientists.

3 A: _____ ?
   B: Yes. Ann is a doctor.

4 A: _____ ?
   B: No. Ellen is a flight attendant. She's not a writer.

5 A: _____ ?
   B: Yes. I am a pilot.

6 A: _____ ?
   B: No. We're not flight attendants. We're pilots.

5 Write six proper nouns and six common nouns. Use capital and lowercase letters correctly.

Proper nouns	Common nouns
1 _____	7 _____
2 _____	8 _____
3 _____	9 _____
4 _____	10 _____
5 _____	11 _____
6 _____	12 _____

1 Write the correct possessive adjectives.

1 Miss Kim is Mr. Smith's student. Mr. Smith is ___her___ teacher.

2 Mr. Smith is Miss Kim's teacher. Miss Kim is _____ student.

3 Mrs. Krauss is John's teacher. Mrs. Krauss is _____ teacher.

4 John is Mrs. Krauss's student. John is _____ student.

5 Are _____ colleagues from Japan? No, they aren't. My colleagues are from Korea.

6 Mr. Bello is _____ teacher. I am _____ student.

7 Jake is not Mrs. Roy's student. He's _____ boss!

8 Mr. Gee is not Jim and Sue's teacher. He's _____ doctor.

2 Complete the sentences about the people. Use He's from, She's from, or They're from.

1 Ms. Tomiko Matsuda: _____ Hamamatsu, Japan.

2 Miss Berta Soliz: _____ Monterrey, Mexico.

3 Mr. and Mrs. Franz Heidelberg: _____ Berlin, Germany.

4 Mr. George Crandall: _____ Victoria, Canada.

5 Ms. Mary Mellon: _____ Melbourne, Australia.

6 Mr. Jake Hild and Ms. Betty Parker: _____ Los Angeles, US.

7 Mr. Cui Jing Wen: _____ Wuhan, China.

8 Ms. Noor Bahjat: _____ Cairo, Egypt.

3 Complete the questions.

1 _____ your name?

2 _____ are you from?

3 _____ his e-mail address?

4 _____ she a student?

5 _____ her phone number?

6 _____ they colleagues?

7 _____ he from China?

8 _____ their first names?

4 Complete each question with the correct possessive adjective.

1 A: What's _____ name?
   B: I'm Mrs. Barker.

2 A: What's _____ last name?
   B: My last name is Crandall.

3 A: What's _____ address?
   B: Mr. Marsh's address is 10 Main Street.

4 A: What's _____ e-mail address?
   B: Ms. Down's e-mail address? It's down5@unet.com.

5 A: What are _____ first names?
   B: They're Gary and Rita.

6 A: What's _____ phone number?
   B: Miss Gu's number is 555-0237.

1 Write the sentences with contractions.

1 Where is the pharmacy? _Where's the pharmacy?_

2 It is down the street. _____

3 It is not on the right. _____

4 What is your name? _____

5 What is your e-mail address? _____

6 She is an architect. _____

7 I am a teacher. _____

8 You are my friend. _____

9 He is her neighbor. _____

10 They are my classmates. _____

2 Complete each sentence with an affirmative or a negative imperative.

1 _____ the bus to the restaurant. _____ walk.

2 _____ the bus to the bank.

3 _____ to the school. It's right over there, on the right.

4 _____ take a taxi to the bank. _____. It's across the street.

3 Complete the questions and answers. Use contractions when possible.

1 A: _____ the pharmacy?
B: The pharmacy? _____ across the street.

2 A: _____ the newsstand?
B: _____ down the street on the right.

3 A: _____ I _____ to the restaurant?
B: No, don't walk there. _____ a taxi.

4 A: _____ do you go to school?
B: Me? I go _____ motorcycle. _____ _____ you?

1 Write questions. Use Who's or Who are and he, she, or they.

1 A: _Who's he_ ?
B: He's my grandfather.

2 A: _____?
B: She's my mother.

3 A: _____?
B: He's Mr. Ginn's grandson.

4 A: _____?
B: They're Ms. Breslin's grandparents.

5 A: _____?
B: She's Sam's wife.

6 A: _____?
B: They're his wife and son.

2 Unscramble the words and write sentences. Use a form of __be__.

1 so / father / my / handsome __My father is so handsome.__

2 brother / very / her / short _____

3 grandchildren / cute / neighbor's / so / my _____

4 his / tall / not / sister / very _____

5 grandfather / very / old / my / not _____

6 girlfriend / pretty / so / brother's / my _____

3 Complete the sentences. Use __have__ or __has__.

1 I _____ two brothers.

2 She _____ one child.

3 They _____ four grandchildren.

4 We _____ six children.

5 You _____ ten brothers and sisters!

6 He _____ three sisters.

4 Complete the questions. Use __How old is__ or __How old are__.

1 _____ your children?

2 _____ his son?

3 _____ her grandchildren?

4 _____ Nancy's sisters?

5 _____ Matt's daughter?

6 _____ their grandmother?

UNIT 5

1 Write a question for each answer. Use __What time__, __What day__, or __When__.

1 __What time is it?_____ It's six thirty.

2 _____ The party is at ten o'clock.

3 _____ The dinner is on Friday.

4 _____ The dance is at eleven thirty on Saturday.

5 _____ The concert is in May.

6 _____ The meeting is at noon.

7 _____ It's a quarter to two.

8 _____ The movie is on Wednesday.

2 Complete each sentence with __in__, __on__, or __at__.

1 The concert is _____ March.

2 The dinner is _____ Friday _____ 6:00.

3 The party is _____ April 4th _____ 9:00.

4 The movie is _____ 3:00 P.M. _____ Tuesday.

5 The game is _____ noon _____ Monday.

6 The meeting is _____ August 10th _____ 9:00 A.M.

1 Complete each sentence with the correct form of the verb.

1 They _____ nice ties at this store.
   have

2 She _____ a long, blue skirt for the party.
   want

3 I _____ my shoes.
   like

4 We _____ clean shirts.
   not have

5 Our children _____ blue pants for school.
   not need

6 _____ short skirts?
   she / like

7 _____ new shoes?
   your wife / need

8 _____ a suit for work?
   I / need

9 Why _____ those old shoes?
   she / like

10 Which shirt _____ for tomorrow?
   you / want

11 _____ this sweater in extra large?
   they / have

2 Answer each question.

1 What clothes do you need? _____

2 Do you need new shoes? _____

3 Why do you need new shoes? _____

4 Do you have a long skirt? _____

5 Do you like pink shirts? _____

6 Do you have a loose sweater? _____

7 Do you like expensive clothes? _____

1 Write the third-person singular form of each verb.

1 shave *shaves* _____
2 brush _____
3 go _____
4 have _____
5 study _____
6 do _____
7 take _____
8 play _____
9 exercise _____
10 visit _____
11 practice _____
12 wash _____
13 come _____
14 change _____
15 make _____
16 get _____
17 comb _____
18 put _____
19 eat _____
20 watch _____
21 clean _____
22 read _____
23 check _____
24 listen _____

2 Complete each question with <u>do</u> or <u>does</u>

1 When _____ you go shopping?

2 What time _____ she make dinner?

3 How often _____ they clean the house?

4 What time _____ your son come home?

5 How often _____ your parents go out for dinner?

6 What time _____ you go to bed?

7 When _____ our teacher check e-mail?

8 How often _____ Alex do the laundry?

3 Unscramble the words and write sentences in the simple present tense.

1 usually / on weekends / go shopping / she *She usually goes shopping on weekends.* _____

2 go dancing / my sisters / on Fridays / sometimes _____

3 in the morning / never / check e-mail / I _____

4 always / my daughter/ to work / take the bus _____

5 we / to school / walk / never _____

6 sometimes / my brother / after work / visit his friends _____

4 Complete each response with <u>do</u> or <u>does</u>.

1 Who takes out the garbage in your house? My daughter _____.

2 Who washes the dishes in your family? I _____.

3 Who makes dinner? My parents _____.

4 Who does the laundry in your house? My brother _____.

5 Who watches TV before dinner? My granddaughter _____.

6 Who takes a bath in the evening? My sister _____.

UNIT 8

1 Write questions with <u>Where</u>.

1 your grandparents / live *Where do your grandparents live?* _____

2 John's friend / go shopping _____

3 her brother / study English _____

4 you / eat breakfast _____

5 they / listen to music _____

6 Rob and Nancy / exercise _____

7 his mother / work _____

8 your brother / do the laundry _____

2 Complete the statements with <u>in</u>, <u>on</u>, <u>at</u>, or <u>to</u>.

1 His house is _____ Barker Street.

2 They work _____ the tenth floor.

3 Ms. Cruz takes the train _____ work.

4 It's _____ 18 Spencer Street.

5 Jack studies French _____ the BTI Institute.

6 Mr. Klein works _____ the hospital.

7 Her office is _____ the fifth floor.

8 She works _____ 5 Main Street.

3 Complete each sentence with **There's** or **There are**.

1 _____ a movie at noon.

2 _____ a concert at 2:00 and a game at 3:00.

3 _____ a bank on the corner of Main and 12th Street.

4 _____ two apartment buildings across the street.

5 _____ bookstores nearby.

6 _____ a pharmacy and a newsstand around the corner.

7 _____ two dressers in the bedroom.

8 _____ three elevators in the Smith Building.

4 Write questions with **Is there** or **Are there**.

1 a dance / this weekend *Is there a dance this weekend?* _____

2 three meetings / this week _____

3 a bank / nearby _____

4 How many / games / this afternoon _____

5 How many / pharmacies / on 3rd Avenue _____

6 How many / parties / this month _____

UNIT 9

1 Write the present participle of the following base forms.

1 rain *raining* _____   15 come _____

2 snow _____   16 wear _____

3 watch _____   17 shop _____

4 eat _____   18 go _____

5 take _____   19 study _____

6 drive _____   20 listen _____

7 check _____   21 wash _____

8 make _____   22 play _____

9 do _____   23 read _____

10 exercise _____   24 clean _____

11 shave _____   25 work _____

12 put _____   26 write _____

13 comb _____   27 talk _____

14 brush _____   28 buy _____

2 Check the sentences that indicate a future plan.

☐ 1 I'm watching TV right now.

☐ 2 Is Marina taking a shower?

☐ 3 On Tuesday I'm working at home.

☐ 4 Where is she going tomorrow night?

☐ 5 Jen's eating dinner.

☐ 6 I'm driving to the mall this afternoon.

☐ 7 I'm studying Arabic this year. My teacher is very good.

☐ 8 Who's making dinner on Saturday?

3 Complete each conversation with the present continuous.

1 A: _What are you doing_?
      you / do

  B: _____ my hair.
      I / wash

2 A: _____ ?
      Where / she / drive

  B: _____ to the bookstore.
      She / go

3 A: _____ the bus?
      Why / he / take

  B: Because _____ .
      it / rain

4 A: _____ at home tonight?
      we / eat

  B: No. _____ out for dinner.
      We / go

5 A: _____ a dress to the party?
      Maya wear

  B: No. _____ a dress. _____ pants.
      she / not wear   She / wear

UNIT 10

1 Complete each question with <u>How much</u> or <u>How many</u>.

1 _____ sugar do you want in your coffee?

2 _____ onions do you need for the potato pancakes?

3 _____ cans of coffee are there on the shelf?

4 _____ meat do you eat every day?

5 _____ loaves of bread do we need for dinner?

6 _____ pepper would you like in your chicken salad?

7 _____ bottles of oil does she need from the store?

8 _____ eggs do you eat every week?

9 _____ oranges are there? I want to make orange juice.

10 _____ pasta would you like?

2 Choose the correct word or phrase to complete each statement. Circle the letter.

1 I _____ English every day.
  a am studying   **b** study

2 We usually _____ the bus to work.
  a are taking   **b** take

3 Annemarie _____ the kitchen now.
  a is cleaning   **b** cleans

4 He really _____ lemonade.
  a is liking   **b** likes

5 This store _____ beautiful clothes.
  a is having   **b** has

6 On Wednesdays I _____ dinner for my parents.
  a am cooking   **b** cook

7 They never _____ coffee.
  a are drinking   **b** drink

8 Our children _____ on weekdays.
  a are watching TV   **b** don't watch TV

1 Complete the conversations with the past tense of <u>be</u>.

1 A: Where _____ Paul and Jackie last night?
   B: I don't know, but they _____ here.

2 A: _____ she at school yesterday?
   B: No. She _____ at home.

3 A: When _____ you in Italy? Last year?
   B: Last year? No, we _____ in Italy last year.
     We _____ thoro in 2005.

4 A: What time _____ the movie?
   B: It _____ at 7:00.

5 A: _____ your parents at home at 10:00 last night?
   B: No. They _____ at a play.

6 A: Who _____ at work on Monday?
   B: Barry and Anne _____. But I _____.

2 First complete each question. Use the simple past tense. Then write an answer.

1 _____ you _____ to work yesterday?
               go
   YOU _____

2 What time _____ you _____ dinner?
                  make
   YOU _____

3 What _____ you _____ for breakfast?
               eat
   YOU _____

4 Who _____ breakfast with you?
        eat
   YOU _____

5 What _____ you _____ this week?
              buy
   YOU _____

1 Write sentences with <u>be</u> or <u>have</u>.

1 Kate's / hair / long / straight _Kate's hair is long and straight._ _____

2 George / short / black / hair _____

3 Harry / long / curly / hair _____

4 Mary's / eyes / blue _____

5 Adam / beard / mustache _____

6 Amy / pretty / eyes _____

2 Complete each sentence with **should** or **shouldn't** and a verb from the box.

1 It's your birthday. You _____ out for dinner!

2 I'm sorry you have a toothache. You _____ a dentist.

3 There's a movie on TV tonight. We _____ it.

4 You have a cold? You _____ today.

5 We have tomatoes, potatoes, and onions. We _____
tomato potato soup for dinner tonight!

6 Pam's taking a shower right now. You _____ back later.

7 Martin has a headache. He _____ soccer tonight.

8 It's time for bed. You _____ undressed.

call
(not) exercise
go
watch
make
(not) play
see
get

UNIT 13

1 Write sentences with the simple present tense and the adverbs **well** or **badly**.

1 my father / sing / really well *My father sings really well.*

2 my mother / cook French food / well _____

3 my grandfather / play the guitar / badly _____

4 my grandmother / sew clothes / very well _____

5 my sister / knit sweaters / well _____

6 my friend / draw pictures / really well _____

7 I / play the violin / badly _____

2 Answer each question. Use short answers with **can** or **can't**.

1 Can you play the piano? _____.

2 Can you ski? _____.

3 Can your parents sing well? _____.

4 Can your friends speak English? _____.

5 Can you draw? _____.

6 Can your father fix things? _____.

3 Complete each sentence. Use **too** and an adjective.

1 I need a new dress. This dress is _____.

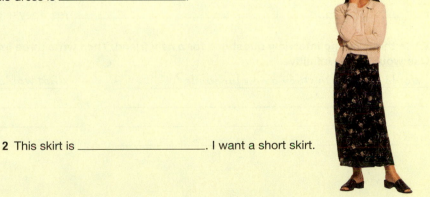

2 This skirt is _____. I want a short skirt.

3 His shirt is _____. He needs size small.

4 I don't want that suit. It's _____.

5 He needs size medium. This shirt is _____.

UNIT 14

1 **Answer the following questions, using <u>be going to</u>.**

1 Are your classmates going to study tonight? _____

2 Are you going to relax this weekend? _____

3 Are you going to exercise today? _____

4 Are you going to make dinner tonight? _____

5 Are you going to move in the next two years? _____

6 Are you going to check your e-mail today? _____

7 Are you going to hang out with your friends or family this weekend?_____

2 **Write a question with <u>be going to</u> for each answer. Don't use the verb <u>do</u>.**

1 _Are you going to go to the movies tonight?_ Yes. I'm going to go to the movies tonight.

2 _____ Yes. They're going to eat in a restaurant after the concert.

3 _____ Yes. Carla's brother is going to go fishing with her.

4 _____ Yes. I'm going to go to work tomorrow.

5 _____ No. He's not going to graduate this year.

6 _____ Yes. They're going to take the bus to school.

3 **Write three <u>yes/no</u> interview questions for a new friend. Then write three information questions.**
Use <u>would like</u> + infinitive.

Would you like to study a new language?   _What would you like to study?_

_____   _____

_____   _____

_____   _____

Top Notch Pop Lyrics

1:30

What Do You Do? [Unit 1]

(CHORUS)
What do you do?
What do you do?

I'm a student.
You're a teacher.
She's a doctor.
He's a nurse.
What about you?
What do you do?
I'm a florist.
You're a gardener.
He's a waiter.
She's a chef.
Do-do-do-do...
That's what we do.
It's nice to meet you.
What's your name?
Can you spell that, please?
Thank you.
Yes, it's nice to meet you, too.

(CHORUS)
We are artists and musicians,
architects, and electricians.
How about you?
What do you do?
We are bankers,
we are dentists,
engineers, and flight attendants.
Do-do-do-do...
That's what we do.
Hi, I'm Linda. Are you John?
No, he's right over there.
Excuse me. Thank you very much.
Good-bye.
Do-do-do-do...
Do-do-do-do...
Do-do-do-do...
Do-do-do-do...

1:46

Excuse Me, Please [Unit 2]

(CHORUS)
Excuse me—please excuse me.
What's your number?
What's your name?
I would love to get to know you,
and I hope you feel the same.

I'll give you my e-mail address.
Write to me at my dot-com.
You can send a note in English
so I'll know
who it came from.
Excuse me—please excuse me.
Was that 0078?
Well, I think the class is starting,
and I don't
want to be late.

But it's really nice to meet you.
I'll be seeing you again.
Just call me on my cell phone
when you're looking for a friend.

(CHORUS)
So welcome to the classroom.
There's a seat right over there.
I'm sorry, but you're sitting in
our teacher's favorite chair!
Excuse me—please excuse me.
What's your number?
What's your name?

2:15

Tell Me All About It [Unit 4]

Tell me about your father.
He's a doctor and he's very tall.
And how about your mother?
She's a lawyer. That's her picture on
the wall.
Tell me about your brother.
He's an actor, and he's twenty-three.
And how about your sister?
She's an artist. Don't you think she looks
like me?

(CHORUS)
Tell me about your family—
who they are and what they do.
Tell me all about it.
It's so nice to talk with you.

Tell me about your family.
I have a brother and a sister, too.
And what about your parents?
Dad's a teacher, and my mother's eyes
are blue.

(CHORUS)
Who's the pretty girl in that photograph?
That one's me!
You look so cute!
Oh, that picture makes me laugh!
And who are the people there, right below
that one?
Let me see ... that's my mom and dad.
They both look very young.

(CHORUS)
Tell me all about it.
Tell me all about it.

2:35

Let's Make a Date [Unit 5]

It's early in the evening—
6:15 P.M.
Here in New York City
a summer night begins.
I take the bus at seven
down the street from City Hall.
I walk around the corner
when I get your call.

(CHORUS)
Let's make a date.
Let's celebrate.
Let's have a great time out.

Let's meet in the Village
on Second Avenue
next to the museum there.
What time is good for you?
It's a quarter after seven.
There's a very good new show
weekdays at the theater.
Would you like to go?

(CHORUS)
Sounds great. What time's the show?
The first one is at eight.
And when's the second one?
The second show's too late.
OK, how do I get there?
The trains don't run at night.
No problem. Take a taxi.
The place is on the right.
Uh-oh! Are we late?
No, we're right on time.
It's 7:58.
Don't worry. We'll be fine!

(CHORUS)

3:15

On the Weekend [Unit 7]

(CHORUS)
On the weekend,
when we go out,
there is always so much joy and laughter.
On the weekend,
we never think about
the days that come before and after.

He gets up every morning.
Without warning, the bedside clock rings
the alarm.
So he gets dressed—
he does his best to be on time.
He combs his hair, goes down the stairs,
and makes some breakfast.
A bite to eat, and he feels fine.
Yes, he's on his way
to one more working day.

(CHORUS)
On Thursday night,
when he comes home from work,
he gets undressed, and if his room's a mess,
he cleans the house. Sometimes he takes
a rest.
Maybe he cooks something delicious,
and when he's done
he washes all the pots and dishes,
then goes to bed.
He knows the weekend's just ahead.

(CHORUS)

🔊 Home Is Where the Heart Is
[Unit 8]

There's a house for everyone
with a garden in the sun.
There's a stairway to the stars.
Where is this house?
It isn't far.

(CHORUS)
Home is where the heart is.
Home is where the heart is.

She lives on the second floor.
There are flowers at her front door.
There's a window with a breeze.
Love and kindness are the keys.

(CHORUS)

There's a room with a view of the sea.
Would you like to go there with me?

(CHORUS)

🔊 Fruit Salad, Baby [Unit 10]

You never eat eggs for breakfast.
You don't drink coffee or tea.
I always end up cooking for you
when you're here with me.
I want to make something delicious,
'cause I like you a lot.
I'm checking my refrigerator,
and this is what I've got:

(CHORUS)
How about a fruit salad, baby—
apples, oranges, bananas too?
Well, here you go now, honey.
Good food coming up for me and you.

Are there any cans or bottles
or boxes on the shelf?
I put my dishes on the counter.
I mix everything well.

(CHORUS)

Chop and drain it.
Slice and dice it.
Mix and serve
with an ounce of love.
Pass your glass.
What are you drinking?
Tell me what dish
I am thinking of?

(CHORUS)

🔊 My Favorite Day [Unit 11]

Last night we walked together.
It seems so long ago.
And we just talked and talked.
Where did the time go?
We saw the moonlit ocean
across the sandy beach.
The waves of summer fell,
barely out of reach.

(CHORUS)
Yes, that was then,
and this is now,
and all I do is think about
yesterday,
my favorite day of the week.

When I woke up this morning,
my feelings were so strong.
I put my pen to paper,
and I wrote this song.
I'm glad I got to know you.
You really made me smile.
My heart belonged to you
for a little while.

(CHORUS)

It was wonderful to be with you.
We had so much to say.
It was awful when we waved good-bye.
Why did it end that way?

(CHORUS)

🔊 She Can't Play Guitar [Unit 13]

She can paint a pretty picture.
She can draw well every day.
She can dance and she can sing,
but she can't play guitar.
She can sew a dress so nicely,
and she does it beautifully.
She can knit a hundred sweaters,
but she can't play guitar.

(CHORUS)
And now it's too late.
She thinks it's too hard.
Her happy smile fades,
'cause she can't play guitar.

She can drive around the city.
She can fix a broken car.
She can be a great mechanic,
but she can't play guitar.

(CHORUS)
And she says,
"Could you please help me?
When did you learn?
Was it hard? Not at all?
Are my hands too small?"
She can cook a meal so nicely
in the kitchen, and there are
lots of things that she does well,
but she can't play guitar.

(CHORUS)

🔊 I Wasn't Born Yesterday [Unit 14]

I went to school and learned the lessons
of the human heart.
I got an education in
psychology and art.
It doesn't matter what you say.
I know the silly games you play.

(CHORUS)
I wasn't born yesterday.
I wasn't born yesterday.

Well, pretty soon I graduated
with a good degree.
It took some time to understand
the way you treated me,
and it's too great a price to pay.
I've had enough, and anyway,

(CHORUS)

So you think I'd like to marry you
and be your pretty wife?
Well, that's too bad, I'm sorry, now.
Grow up and get a life!
It doesn't matter what you say.
I know the silly games you play.

(CHORUS)